The Jungle Doctor Series, No. 2.

JUNGLE DOCTOR ON SAFARI

Books by Dr. Paul White

The JUNGLE DOCTOR Series

JUNGLE DOCTOR
JUNGLE DOCTOR ON SAFARI
JUNGLE DOCTOR OPERATES
JUNGLE DOCTOR ATTACKS WITCHCRAFT
JUNGLE DOCTOR'S ENEMIES
JUNGLE DOCTOR MEETS A LION
JUNGLE DOCTOR TO THE RESCUE
JUNGLE DOCTOR'S CASE-BOOK
JUNGLE DOCTOR AND THE WHIRLWIND
EYES ON JUNGLE DOCTOR

JUNGLE DOCTOR'S PROGRESS
JUNGLE DOCTOR PANORAMA
A magnificent pictorial record
JUNGLE DOCTOR LOOKS FOR TROUBLE

JUNGLE DOCTOR GOES WEST
JUNGLE DOCTOR STINGS A SCORPION
JUNGLE DOCTOR HUNTS BIG GAME
JUNGLE DOCTOR ON THE HOP
JUNGLE DOCTOR'S CROOKED DEALINGS
JUNGLE DOCTOR SPOTS A LEOPARD
JUNGLE DOCTOR PULLS A LEG
JUNGLE DOCTOR SEES RED

JUNGLE DOCTOR'S FABLES
JUNGLE DOCTOR'S MONKEY TALES
JUNGLE DOCTOR'S TUG-OF-WAR
JUNGLE DOCTOR'S HIPPO HAPPENINGS

PAUL WHITE

JUNGLE DOCTOR ON SAFARI

With Thirty-eight Illustrations
by HARRY SWAIN and LOLA JONES

THE PATERNOSTER PRESS

ISBN: 0 85364 053 X

First Published (in Australia)		1943
Published in this Uniform Edition		1950
Second Impression	*May,*	1951
Third Impression	*February,*	1953
Fourth Impression	*October,*	1953
Fifth Impression	*October,*	1954
Sixth Impression	*April,*	1956
Seventh Impression	*March,*	1958
Eighth Impression	*September,*	1960
Ninth Impression	*February,*	1963
Tenth Impression	*October,*	1965
Eleventh Impression	*March,*	1970

AUSTRALIA:
Emu Book Agencies Pty., Ltd.,
511, Kent Street, Sydney, N.S.W.

CANADA:
Home Evangel Books Ltd.,
25, Hobson Avenue, Toronto, 16

NEW ZEALAND:
G. W. Moore, Ltd.,
3, Campbell Road, P.O. Box 24053
Royal Oak, Auckland, 6

SOUTH AFRICA:
Oxford University Press
P.O. Box 1141
Thibault House, Thibault Street
Cape Town

Made and Printed in Great Britain for The Paternoster Press Paternoster House 3 Mount Radford Crescent Exeter Devon by Cox & Wyman Limited London Fakenham, Reading

CONTENTS

CHAPTER I

A CAR, A CATARACT AND THE COW'S HUSBAND

"HIGHER, Samson!"

"Half an inch up!"

"More!"

"A little more!"

"Right!!"

I lay at full length under the old box-bodied Ford.

From my vantage point, I could see Tanganyika from an unusual angle. On one side, set wide apart, were two stalwart African legs. Samson was using his great strength to lift the whole of the left side of the car off the ground while I slipped the jack into place. I watched his muscles relax as he gently lowered the chassis. He grunted, and moved off to get the spare.

Directly in front lay the apology for a road. Framed between the front wheels was a typical picture of Central African life. There was a squat Gogo house, mud-and-wattle walled, with a bundle of grass and some pumpkins and gourds on the roof, and beyond it a small boy, armed with a knobbed stick, was watching a few hungry-looking hump-backed cattle and a mixed assortment of goats and fat-tailed sheep.

The quiet of the tropical midday was broken by the shrill whistle of the Tanganyika Express, labouring inland on its 700-mile journey from Dar-es-Salaam on the

Indian Ocean coast to the Great Lakes. The unusual sound startled hundreds of ibis, who had been sedately stalking amongst the young millet crop, picking up caterpillars. With a swirl of wings, they flew into the air and skimmed around in great circles. Through a break in the thornbush we watched the train, its third-class carriages packed with Africans, Indians and Arabs. Limp-looking Europeans gazed out at the wide sweep of the Central Plain. The train rattled away into the desert.

Samson blew up the punctured tube and placed it on a patch of smooth dust. Carefully he lifted it, and a small crater in the dust showed him where the puncture was. He marked it quickly, and, running his hand round

inside the tyre cover, deftly produced an iron-hard two-inch thorn that had caused the puncture. Ten minutes later we were on safari again.

We negotiated four rivers, and crossed the railway line before driving through Kikombo, with its market place and dingy, mud-brick shops. Beyond the town was a stretch of country that in the eight months' dry season was brown, barren plain covered with stunted undergrowth and straggly thornbush, but in the rains it was utterly changed. There had been heavy thunder showers, and the whole face of the land was a mass of blue, yellow and pink convolvulus growing broadcast. Tall native hollyhocks, purple, yellow and red, grew in profusion on a hill that sloped down to the river bank. The river itself was a quarter of a mile wide, and its bed was hard, wet sand, since only the night before it had been a raging torrent as the storm water had rushed down from the hills on the horizon.

Before attempting to cross, Samson pulled up and pointed with his chin to the far bank, where the road ended in a sheer drop of six feet to the river level. Thousands of tons of soil had been eroded in the flood of storm water which had turned a quarter of a mile stretch of sand into a raging torrent. He and Daudi took hoes from the back of the car and set to work to level down the bank sufficiently for us to get on our way.

I was about to help with a spade, when I saw three cattle being driven up the river bank by an old man and two small boys. The old man peered at me. He shaded his eyes, and all at once his face broke into a smile, and he hurried across to me.

"*Mbukwa*, Bwana."

"*Mbukwa*," I replied.

Firmly we shook hands, and I recognized him as one of my star patients. His feet and legs had been extensively burnt, and both of his eyes bore the mark of cataract operations.

"Well, Mulewa," I said, "how are you?"

"Mulewa?" he said. "My name is not Mulewa!"

"Oh, yes, it is," I replied. "Did I not treat your burns when you were blind and walked into the fire? And did I not operate on your eyes and give you back your sight?"

"Yes, Bwana, you did all that, but my name is not Mulewa"—and then he laughed. "It used to be, but now it is Benjamin. Behold!" From round his neck he took a little wooden bottle, pulled out the cork, and shook into his hand two little bits of tissue that looked like shop-soiled split peas. They were his eye lenses. He thrust these at me, and said:

"For ten years, Bwana, those stopped me from seeing. I could not get rid of them, nor could the witch-doctor, nor my relatives, but you did with your little knife, and, behold, I understood how Jesus could take away sin, the cataract of the soul. So I became a Christian. Now my name is Benjamin, and I am taking these three cows to Buigiri as my thank-offering to God."

Very carefully he put his cataracts back in the bottle, and hung it round his neck again.

"Truly," said he, "you preached much better with your knife than with your tongue."

It was only the day before that Samson had reminded me of a famous sermon that I had once preached, when, in all sincerity, I had told the congregation how, in the jungle, I had seen buffaloes leaping from limb to limb, and agilely swinging themselves about by their tails. When you realize that in Swahili *nyani* means a monkey, and *nvati* is a buffalo, you can understand how mistakes arise.

"How are you, these days, Benjamin, have you strength in your body?"

"Yes, Bwana, much strength, but I have small pain in my chest."

He unwrapped a grey cotton blanket from his shoulder and seated himself on a boulder in the middle of the river.

"Bwana, if you have your *cihulicizizo* (stethoscope) I would have great joy if you would listen to my chest."

I tapped and listened.

It is useless to ask an African to say "ninety-nine" during this proceeding, so I had chosen "*Ngombe*" to take its place. This word means "cow" in Chigogo, the local language.

The old man was taking deep breaths, and then saying *ngombe* while I listened intently. Little did I realize that, before the day was out, I would have real trouble with that word *cow.* I reassured the old man, and promised him medicine later on in the day at the hospital. He said farewell, and drove his cows on. Before long, we had levelled down the river bank sufficiently to continue our safari.

Nearing Buigiri, we saw numbers of people coming along, each driving a hump-backed cow towards the church. It is more usual to see people carrying grain in great conical baskets—the women placing them expertly on their heads, while the men carry them on their shoulders—but to-day it was a matter of cattle.

We pulled up outside the hospital. The old African clergyman and the village school teacher hurried forward to shake hands.

"*Mbukwa*, Bwana," said they.

"*Ale Mbukwenyi*," I replied.

"Bwana, there are big doings this year. Our people have decided that, as a thank-offering to God for good crops, each household will bring a cow."

I could hear behind the church the stamping and lowing of cattle. The service of offering their gifts to God was a very impressive one. My mind was full of schemes. I could see all sorts of possibilities. There would be a herd of some forty cattle, and, although these hardy desert creatures produced only a pint or so of milk a day, we could do a lot with forty pints. The children at hospital could get fresh milk daily—this would strike a death blow at rickets. Then I thought of the calves, and of the change a little veal would be to the usual routine of tough, twopenny Tanganyikan chicken. All sorts of rosy ideas rushed through my brain.

I buttonholed the old clergyman and said:

"Pastor, this is a splendid thing. With all these

ngombe (cows) we will be able to make the children strong, and help them to overcome disease. Then we can teach the people how to milk the cows in a clean way."

The old man covered his face with his hands, but I still kept on.

"We will teach them to sterilize their buckets. We will have a model dairy. Indeed, this is a great forward step in improving the welfare of the tribe."

He did his best to cover his smiles.

The school teacher had a severe bout of coughing, and Daudi hurriedly went to fill the radiator.

Samson stood his ground, but his eyes twinkled merrily. He turned to me and said:

"Have you inspected the herd, Bwana?"

"Not yet, Samson. Why?"

"Well, let's go and have a look at it."

The teacher's cough must have been infectious, because the pastor was coughing, and tears were running out of his eyes.

Daudi was filling a kerosene tin with water on the other side of the Mission House, and I could hear roar upon roar of laughter coming from that direction.

I looked at my companion questioningly:

"What's up, Samson? What's the joke?"

We had just come within sight of the thornbush enclosure and the cattle inside it.

"What are they laughing at? What have I said wrong this time?"

"Nothing, Bwana, your language is all right, but perhaps you do not yet quite understand the word '*Ngombe*'."

"But I do, Samson. '*Ngombe*' means 'Cow'."

Then I looked at the beasts, and light dawned.

Samson saw my look of amazement, and burst out laughing.

"You see, Bwana, '*Ngombe*' does not only mean a cow. It also means the husband of a cow, and, behold, Bwana, are they not all husbands?"

I sat down on the running-board of the car and laughed and laughed and laughed.

CHAPTER II

SUKUMA

DAUDI struggled into my room with a kerosene tin in each hand, and poured the water they contained into a small tin tub. It was definitely not big enough to accommodate half of me at a time, but it was the sort of bath that one has on safari. Daudi grinned as he went through the door:

"Bwana, that is a tub with a weak bottom. When you sit in it, it makes loud noises." It certainly did. In the middle of my struggles an urgent voice came at the door:

"*Hodi*, Bwana?"

"*Lindile*" (wait a bit), I cried, girded on a towel and went to the window. "What's up?"

"A sick one, Bwana."

It was well after dark, but, by the light of a young moon, I could see an African ambulance—a pole, with a blanket pinned to it with thorns.

"Tell them to go on to the hospital," I said, "I will be down in five minutes."

Samson met me outside the door.

"*Ehh!*" said he, "three months at home—same old story. The witch-doctors are defeated, the child is half dead, and so they come to us. It is a little girl, Bwana, perhaps she is ten. Her legs are drawn up, so"—he sat on the ground and put his knees under his chin—"and she has ulcers such as we have never seen before."

We walked together to the out-patients' room, its mud roof sprouting grass, and there, huddled on a blanket on the floor, was a wasted, terrified little girl. I bent forward to look at her. Under each of her knees was an ulcer larger than the palm of your hand. She was covered with skin disease and sores, and had a patch on her forearm that looked like leprosy.

I ordered treatment and dressings, and, after a long discussion, her relatives agreed to leave her at the hospital and later to carry her over the hills to Mvumi, where operations would be necessary to straighten her legs. I watched the Sister and the African nurse carefully dressing her ghastly ulcers, and I shuddered to think what that poor child must have suffered in a mud hut, lying on a cow-skin, covered by a threadbare blanket.

At dawn next morning we were ready to move on to our next hospital. We waved good-bye to the staff of this C.M.S. medical outpost, and drove down the hill towards the scarcely-defined track which was the main road to the coast.

There was a defiant bellow from the cattle *boma*.

The track led us through a thornbush forest. At times we appeared to be actually in a tunnel, as the branches of the trees met overhead. On one side of the road was a small lake, its shallows a mass of water-lilies of many different colours. In it were hundreds of birds. Ducks and knob-billed geese swam away, while egrets flew up in a white cloud as we passed. The sun beat down powerfully, hardening the slippery road which wound its way down a boulder-strewn hill and zigzagged towards a place which, in the rainy season, was a river two miles wide, and, in the dry, was a mere depression between the hills. It was called the Chinyasungwe River.

I was thinking of a day the year before when the Bishop was on safari. His car had been stuck in the black soil and caught by flood waters. He, and his car boy, Jacob, had tied his bogged car to a tree and watched the water rise till only the hood was visible. Then they had to wade miles by the light of a hurricane lantern, and miles more without it, after the African lad had slipped into a deep water-hole.

My happy memories of other people's misfortunes were cut short by a gasp from Daudi. With his chin he pointed to a group of rocks not thirty yards away from us. There, looking down at the car in a most benign fashion, were three lions. One of them got to his feet and stretched. Fortunately, the black soil, though sticky, was firm enough to allow us to slip and skid our way along the road and leave the lions to their thoughts and digestion. Over the plain beyond us were giraffe and buck grazing, and later we saw a small herd of zebra.

Apart from some rather bewildering skids, nothing eventful happened, until we climbed a hill that was bone dry. A mile or so ahead a great cloud of red dust was rising up in the still air. We stopped to investigate, walking along a narrow path through the undergrowth. We came upon an animated scene—a native dance, where everything was done with the utmost noise and enthusiasm. I stood watching from behind a great baobab tree for a minute, and then unslung my camera. Suddenly, one of the principal dancers in the centre of a ring of sweating, stamping, chanting figures leapt on to the broad shoulders of two of his companions. I moved closer and focused carefully. The dancer flung his arms up, the ostrich plumes in his mud head-dress quivering.

"Quick, Bwana, quick, take it now," whispered Samson.

The shutter clicked. It was a splendid study. The dancer gleamed with sweat, the fox tails tied to his ankles showed up well at this angle, as also did the

bright blue-bag colour round his mouth and red ochre round his eyes. He proceeded to render a species of solo to the accompaniment of stamping, a series of "*Aya's*," and piercing blasts on a postman's whistle.

Samson pulled my arm, and I saw coming towards me the Chief. He was an old friend, and a grateful patient. We went through elaborate greetings, and then he said:

"Did you take pictures, Bwana? Have you the dance trapped in your little black box?"

I showed him the camera. By now the smell and the dust were becoming rather overpowering, so I walked back to the car with the Chief. I took the precaution of leaving him four aspirin, for I felt sure the noise of that day's festivities would produce a severe headache. A quarter of an hour of ear-splitting whistles and the earth-shaking thump of a thousand feet was more than enough for me.

True to form, the old car refused to start. The Chief

ordered a dozen of the dancers to push. They yelled with delight, and broke into a sort of chanty, each line ending with a shout—"*Sukuma!*"

"What does '*sukuma*' mean, Samson?" I asked.

"'Push,' Bwana."

"Right! From now on the car shall be called 'Sukuma'."

As if in protest, the engine started, and we swung round a corner and out of view of a most amusing impromptu dance, illustrating our recent predicament. I heard them give a final "*Sukuma*" as we moved along the last lap of our journey to Mpwapwa.

CHAPTER III

CONFUSION TO THE KING OF BEASTS

It was just noon when we arrived at the little Church Missionary Society House, on the side of the historic Mpwapwa Mountain, overlooking mile after mile of rolling plain. The staff from the nearby hospital ran out to greet us. I could see a dozen patients waiting for treatment, and I knew that before the day was out the news would have spread and their ranks would be well over the hundred.

I was welcomed to lunch by the missionary in charge, who had been a famous hockey blue during his university days.

"You judged your arrival well, my boy," said he. "The Agricultural Officer has invited us out to dinner and promised that we would have neither chicken nor spinach. I have accepted for you already. By the way, I have got a splendid lion story to tell you, although perhaps it might be better if we left the recounting of it to our host, since it was I who shot the lion."

There was a clamour from outside, which I knew meant work, so I went up to the hospital and spent the afternoon with stethoscope and syringe. Samson and Daudi were busy washing bottles. It seemed to me that everybody had a severe pain, which in no way impaired their cheerfulness. Those that were real, I dealt with; those that were not, were given a card with "Mist. Mag.

Sulph." written on it. In the late afternoon we started to dispense. Sitting outside the little grass-roofed, mud-walled hospital, carefully I weighed out and measured various drugs. Before sundown, I had dispensed ten gallons of six different coloured medicines.

Samson and I carried the bottles back to the dispensary, with the aid of two of the nurses, who insisted on carrying them balanced on their heads. I had shivers down my spine as I watched them walk unconcernedly along with great bottles of cough mixture on the top of their closely-shaven heads.

After sunset, I set out with my friend, the Padre, and we walked the mile to the main Government centre, where we were to dine with the Agricultural Officer. The road led through a particularly dark place. My companion shone his torch on the track.

"It was last week, Doctor, that I shot the lion, nine feet from tip to tip. It was a . . ."

From behind us came a queer sort of whinnying grunt. I gripped the Padre's arm. "What was that?" But he only laughed. "That's nothing more than an old hippo that wanders around this part of the world each evening. He has come up from the lake over there."

After an excellent dinner, we moved out into the mosquito-wired veranda to drink coffee. The air was fragrant with the scent of frangipanni. My host lifted his cup:

"This is by way of being a celebration. Here's cheers to the Padre and confusion to the king of beasts and all his relatives."

"Spin us the yarn," I begged. We settled down in easy chairs, and he commenced:

"It started a month ago, when my head boy complained that one of our champion steers had been killed. In a week, two more had mysteriously disappeared. I went round to investigate after I came back from safari, and Yohanna took me to see the place:

"'Bwana,' said he, 'there are lions everywhere'—and there certainly were. There were lions' footprints in my wife's flower-beds out there; they were even on the front door-step, and many of the people in the native villages were too frightened to come out of their homes after dark, and so the Padre and I formed a council of war. We planned a lion hunt, and between us, hit on an idea. We would leave the stage set, the cattle in their usual kraal, and we would hide behind a huge baobab tree, each armed with a sporting rifle and a shot-gun, loaded with ball. It was quite an easy matter planning it, but, when a couple of hours after dark the next evening, six of us—the Padre here, myself, and four Africans—went to our battle stations behind that huge tree, well, I frankly admit it was a bit eerie. Two of the Africans went to the kraal to act as a forward scouting party. We both checked up the loading of our rifles and guns. The cartridges in both barrels of the guns were loaded with a lump of lead as big as a marble, and, as you know, when these are fired at close quarters they will blow a hole as big as a soup plate in any animal.

"The crickets chirped in the grass. The mosquitoes swarmed around. They had a very real interest in the proceedings. Away beyond the cattle-yard a hyena howled. The cattle stirred restively, and, as the moon came over the thornbush-covered hill, away in the distance, a lion roared throatily.

"We peered expectantly, but in the dim light we could see nothing. We rubbed a little chalk on the sights of the rifles. You couldn't afford to miss when you were only a few yards away from an extremely hostile lion. One whack of his paw sets the obituary notices in motion.

"The hum of the insects continued, but no further sound from the lion. There was something uncanny about watching that hill down which we knew the lion was coming stealthily. Death lurked there, and yet everything looked peaceful and quiet. Behind us, the plains were bathed in moonlight, and the midnight breeze stirred the leaves in the most soothing fashion.

"I looked across at the Padre:

"'Midnight,' he growled, 'and these mosquitoes are eating me. I wish I were in bed'—and I agreed with him. I was getting cramped. The minutes crawled by, and the insects crawled with them. Everything was silent, when suddenly, close behind us, a hyena gave its ghastly laugh. A sleepy African stumbled to his feet, fell over the legs of his companion, and crashed into a bush of nettles. The hyena slunk off.

"'*Aya, eh, aya, yaya, gwe,*' said the African as he tenderly rubbed his damaged anatomy.

"We chuckled.

"Then things became dull again. I glanced at my luminous watch.

"'Two o'clock, Padre. We'll give it another quarter of an hour. If it doesn't turn up then, well—bed.'

"Ten minutes passed. The Padre sat up and stretched. He was in the middle of a most satisfying yawn when one of the Africans grasped his shoulder and pointed at a spot just beyond the cattle-yard.

"Sleep was forgotten. I was on one side of the tree, the Padre on the other. Each of us peered cautiously round his particular side. There, framed in the door of the kraal, were the enormous shoulders and black mane of a veritable king among lions. The moonlight made him look even bigger.

"The cattle snorted with terror and tried to break their way through the thornbush hedge. The lion's breathing was clearly audible in the quiet of the night. Sedately,

and without hurry, he moved into the enclosure. According to plan, I shone my torch on to the great shaggy head. The eyes glared blood red, his mouth opened in an ugly snarl. This was the pre-arranged sign to fire.

"The Padre fired. The lion snorted, half rose on its hind legs, and came down again, staggering. For a moment I thought it was crouching to spring. I gripped the shot-gun loaded with ball. I had it to my shoulder.

But there was no need to touch the trigger, the great beast crashed to the ground, stone dead.

"We moved out to have a look at it, and were discussing whether it was nine feet from tip to tip, or longer, when a stealthy movement in the darkness made us grasp our rifles again. I thought it was a second lion, but it turned out to be nothing more ferocious than a jackal!"

The Agricultural Officer poured himself another cup of coffee, and I applauded the story.

Then we listened to the B.B.C. news. Big Ben boomed through the loud-speaker. Hyenas howled outside. It was an unusual combination of sound.

As the Padre and I walked home up the hill, the moon was at the full. Vague shadows crossed the road. I could see a black mane in every swaying thornbush. I felt certain something was lurking round each corner, and my heart almost stopped still when there was a crashing in the tall grass beyond the Mission House and a peculiar grunting sound. But this time I was reassured. On the skyline outlined by the moon, was the silhouette of the hippo.

CHAPTER IV

LEOPARD IN THE BLACK-OUT

SOMEONE was opening the door of my room. It was still dark. I peered through the mosquito curtains:

"*Hodi?*" said a voice.

"*Karibu,*" I replied.

In walked the odd-job man of the hospital.

"*Uze ku hospitali, mbera!*" (Come to the hospital, Bwana, quickly!)

I groped for my clothes, following him at the double, doing up buttons as I ran.

In the little grass-roofed ward we worked at high pressure by the light of a hurricane lantern, and in half an hour three lives had been saved. It had been an exacting time, but worth it. The old African nurse could have dealt with the mother by herself, but the twins could hardly have survived. I was amazed at the efficiency of old Mwendwa. She had kept her head admirably in conditions that necessitated the utmost coolness. The babies were being bathed by a junior nurse, and were making it very obvious that they were alive. I dubbed them 'Sing' and 'Song' on the spot. As I felt the mother's pulse, she whispered:

"Bwana, all four of my children have died; they were born in the bush, but these two will live."

Mwendwa grunted: "Feed them as I tell you and

they'll live, but give them porridge and they'll die, like the others."

As I walked back to the house the sun rose over the hill where the lion had been shot.

"Up early, Doctor," laughed my friend, as he poured me a cup of tea.

"Yes, Padre, but three lives saved before breakfast is a pretty good start for any day."

I planned to leave well before midday, but I had to deal first with a case of snake-bite and then with a leaky radiator. It was four o'clock when we waved good-bye and moved off on the twenty-mile drive to Kongwa.

We stopped at an Indian shop to buy three cases of petrol, and then my eye alighted on some packets of chocolate. I debated in my mind whether this was a luxury or not. Deciding that it was not, I bought a packet.

The road wound at the foot of the hills. It was very slippery, and we had a number of rather uncomfortable skids. I drove carefully, as we had a very precious cargo. At Mpwapwa I had picked up my wife and small son—a baby in arms at the time—and was taking them to Kongwa to spend the rest of their holidays.

I looked rather anxiously at my watch. It was half-past four. We should be at Kongwa easily before dark, but you can never be sure of what will happen next on safari in Tanganyika. We had just come level with the place where I had watched the native dance two days before, when I saw a man running frenziedly towards the road waving. I pulled up:

"Bwana, the *Mutemi* wants you urgently," he gasped breathlessly. With a groan, I followed the messenger, to find the Chief, with a number of the old men of the tribe, watching an unfortunate woman on the floor, whose whole body was quivering in the most alarming fashion. Her eyes rolled, her cheeks blew in and out, and her ample lips were never still.

"Bwana," said the Chief, "this woman has *machisi*, the devil is upon her."

"I have a medicine for that," I replied, with a smile, and proceeded to take a bottle from a pocket in the side of the car. The woman blew her cheeks in and out in the most terrifying fashion, and wagged her head from side to side, until I felt sure it must come off.

I handed Daudi the bottle. Carefully he took out the

cork, went close to the woman, and blew the fumes gently towards her. One moment her eyes were rolling in her head, and her body quivering, the next she had stopped, let out one terrific cough, and sat on the ground exhausted but normal.

The Chief and some of the old men looked on in amazement.

"*Yah*," they said, "we have never seen anything like that. That's medicine!"

Daudi blew a little in their direction. They clapped their hands over their mouths. "Eh, it's strong." For at least five minutes they talked excitedly amongst themselves. Then the Chief said: "What medicine was it, Bwana? Is it a secret? Is it one of the things that only doctors know about? Perhaps I should not ask you to tell me?"

"Oh, no, *Mutemi*, that's all right. There is nothing secret about our hospital and our medicines. This is a medicine I keep in the car, just in case we meet a lion."

"*Yah*, it must be strong. Are not rifles better?"

"Game licences cost hundreds of shillings, so I protect myself in other ways. I guarantee the fiercest lion would be discouraged if he got a bottleful of that medicine in his face."

"*Yah*," said Daudi, "would he not cough! Truly, ammonia is a good medicine."

There was still half an hour of light when we set out on the final stage of our journey—or, rather, what I thought was to be the final stage. I had just turned off on the narrow, bumpy track that led to Kongwa hospital when I heard the sickly hiss of a puncture. The sun was setting behind a cone-shaped hill, which the locals say is haunted. We made record time changing the wheel, and on we went again. The limbs of the thorn-bush that met overhead intensified the gloom, and I switched on the headlights. Nothing happened. The baby was hungry, and started to cry. I sprang out, lifted the bonnet, and tried to check up on the wiring system. From the back of the car I produced an electric torch, but in the half light I tripped over a stick and fell, shattering the bulb of the torch. Now there were no means of inspecting the interior of the dilapidated old car. I dared not have an open light because of the strong smell of petrol. I thought for a moment, and then called Daudi and Samson, and, before long, we had a blazing fire of dried thornbush.

My wife got out and walked up and down the road with the infant. She was still within a score of yards of the car admiring the silhouette of the hills against the deep purple of the dying sunset. She called to me: "There is something making a peculiar noise here." Samson listened intently: "*Bibi*, run! Come back quickly, *Chuwi*!" "It's a leopard, Mary!" I gasped. She hurried back into the fire-light. Out there in the gloom we could see something moving stealthily in the darkness.

I felt that things were not in good shape. I couldn't trace the lighting fault, and here we were in the dark, with a whole menagerie of Tanganyikan animals wandering around and exhibiting an inquiring turn of mind. Together we knelt in the fire-light, and simply I told God of our plight, and asked His help. I saw the family safely seated in the front of the car. The infant was asleep. The mosquitoes were hovering around the place, and, for all I knew, each one of them might have been malarial.

I tried to light up the engine by using the rear view mirror, which reflected the flickering light from the fire, and then I found the difficulty. I repaired the broken wire, and wrapped it round with a piece of sticking plaster, only to find that the fuse had blown. That should have presented no difficulty, but for the fact that someone at Mpwapwa had "borrowed" the box in which they were kept. Once again it seemed we were to be stuck out there in the jungle amongst the menagerie for the night. Under my breath, I prayed for help. Suddenly I felt hungry, and thought of the chocolate; here was the answer to the problem. I had been in two minds about buying that chocolate, but unquestionably the whole matter had been planned by a God who pays attention to minute detail. I took some of the silver paper wrapping and twisted it round a stick to make an impromptu fuse and slipped it into the clip. A flick of the switch, and the road ahead of us was lighted up.

"*Yah*," said Samson, "*Swanu*" (good), and from beside me I heard my wife saying, "Thank God." I called the African lads round me, and together we did.

I have never appreciated so much as that night the value of light. In an hour we were at Kongwa. It is not an imposing town, lying miles from the railway, a group of buildings in the hollow of the hills, but it was a place which, that day, was to receive news that made it world-famous.

From the back of the car I produced the mail bag. The Nursing Sister, who, by herself, dealt with that Medical Mission outpost, put it aside until she had arranged for my wife and small son, and then she opened her mail. Enthusiasm hardly describes our feelings when we read that this little C.M.S. Hospital that had cost less than a hundred pounds to build had gained the Imperial Baby Week Shield against Empire-wide competition.

CHAPTER V

PUNCTURES PERMITTING AND A TRAGEDY AT BEREGA

I HAD planned to arrive at Berega at noon. It was seventy-two miles, and I thought, punctures permitting, we would do it comfortably, but here we were, still within sight of Kongwa, and it was ten o'clock.

Samson was mending our eleventh puncture:

"*Kah,*" said he, "why these people will cut the branches off thorn trees and leave them in the middle of the road, I do not know. Five thorns in that tyre, six in this!"

I walked round the car and looked at the front wheel on the driver's side. It, too, was flat. Samson looked up and laughed.

"We'll reach Berega, perhaps, to-morrow, Bwana; I'll fix them up. You go and take pictures."

I helped him to get the jack under the axle, and then strolled down the hill towards the village market. This place, which the locals called Soko, always intrigued me. I could never pass the long queue of gourds, clay pots, calabashes and kerosene tins, without smiling. As each particular vessel came near to the hand of the red-fezzed Swahili who controlled the water-tap, woman after woman would break away from the crowd that squatted in the shade of an umbrella tree. Two or three small girls moved up the vessels continually. The fortunate ones would unwind a length of cloth from behind their shapely bodies and, coiling it, quoit fashion, would put it on their closely-shaven heads and balance their calabashes. Then they would rearrange the babies on their backs, shout farewell, and set out for home, which might be two or twelve miles away across the plain.

I took half a dozen photos and discussed the crops with the market master. Our old car announced its coming long before it was in view, with a series of rattles and bumps. It was eleven o'clock when I scrambled on board, and we set out on our journey, driving for miles under the shade of granite-cragged mountains. We passed women going home from the water supply. As they heard us coming, they would grasp their precious burdens and hurry off the track, waving and smiling, as we passed.

We started to climb and went through the foothills past Rubeho, which boasted the usual group of Indian shops, then came a steep, unfenced mountain pass and a series of red-soil switch-backs. The country became heavily timbered. The monkey population was in its element. In places the grass was higher than the car. Imposing mountain ranges loomed up on each side of the road. There were sugar-cane gardens beside mountain

streams, and the houses were built with conical grass roofs. The people spoke a different language from those we had greeted half an hour before, and I knew we were near our journey's end. In front of us, high up on a tree, was a signboard, which read:

C.M.S., BEREGA,
3 MILES

"*Kah,*" said Samson, "that signpost is high up."

I laughed. "Yes, I have heard a story of that. When it was lower down, people on safari would pull it down and use the wood to make musical instruments, but up there . . ." Samson smiled. "You would need to be *Nhwiga* (the giraffe himself) to get at that."

We drove over an exceedingly rough track through waving grass lands to enter an avenue of frangipanni. The school children hurried out and clapped their hands in welcome. With a screech of brakes, we pulled up in front of the hospital, a grass-thatched, mud-walled place whose only claim to luxury was a concrete floor. It cost £25 to build. I shook hands with all the staff, and, leaving them to unpack, went off to the Mission House. I was determined to have some sleep that

night, for I knew from experience what the next day would hold.

Early next morning I walked down to the hospital with the Australian nurse who ran it, single-handed.

"Goodness, Doctor, we are glad to see you. There will be hundreds of people waiting for you."

When we got to the hospital, we found that it was no overstatement. Squatting all over the place were people who had come for medical aid. It is the custom of these people to bring a "thank you" for any medicine they receive—either a couple of eggs, some beans, a corn-cob or two, a bundle of firewood, or a paw-paw. As I sat at a table contrived from an old packing-box, I saw case after case. Each one would first hand me his "thank you" and then explain his symptoms. Things were not

made easier by the fact that they spoke a dialect with which I was only partially familiar. There was the usual run of coughs, pains in the chest, sore eyes and ears, scratches and bumps and bruises. There was, of course, malaria in abundance, tick fever, hook-worm, bilharzia, and a host of more vague tropical illnesses.

The African nurses poured out doses of medicines industriously. Others put drops into eyes, ears and noses, while still others expertly applied ointment and bandages, and, in a little grass hut boasting a glass window, sat an African boy with his eye glued to a microscope, carefully unravelling the problem of the tropical fever.

There was a batch of half a dozen people waiting especially. One old woman had been blind for years, and she was pathetically anxious for me to remove her cataracts. I made a careful investigation, and agreed to do it that afternoon. The whole situation bristled with difficulties. I would have to operate on the out-patients' table, with a couple of petrol boxes put at the end to make it long enough. The patient had had little preparation for the operation, but one had to take risks when making a hurried tour of the seven hospitals, which was part of my job in Central Tanganyika. After the old woman came three folk with enormous ulcers. All had been under treatment for six months or more. Their legs had reached the stage when skin-grafts would be most effective.

"I will do these chaps, too, this afternoon, Sister, and we can fix up that child with the broken arm. It has been broken three weeks, you think? It will be a nasty job out here without an X-ray, and all that swelling makes it extremely hard to feel anything. That will keep us busy for the whole afternoon."

A thin mountain mist came down, not improving the light in the out-patients' room, which we used as a theatre. At the door stood an African nurse with a flit-spray. She dealt most effectively with any inquisitive fly or wasp. Above my head was stretched a sheet to act as an auxiliary ceiling. Often bits of grass or debris would fall from the roof. This was not particularly desirable in the middle of a surgical procedure!

The old woman was the first job. She did everything she was told, and within a few moments, the operation was over, and she was being carried to the ward, clutching in a piece of cotton wool the lens of her eye, which I had removed, and which had been blocking her vision for so many years.

Then I anæsthetized the child with the broken arm. While the last of three skin grafts were being bandaged by the Sister, the local African school teacher put his head round the door.

"Bwana, may I watch?"

I nodded.

He was most intrigued with the proceedings until he got a whiff of ether.

"*O-o-o-o-f*," he said. '*A-a-a-a-hg!* A very powerful smell!"

"It's sleep medicine," I replied.

"*Yah*," said he, holding his nose, "I want to remain awake."

The patient gradually slipped into unconsciousness, and then the arm could be manipulated into position. Carefully I felt along the lines of the bones. After a full ten minutes of manipulation I looked up:

"The broken ends of bone seem in decent alignment now, Sister. Give me the plaster-of-Paris bandages, please."

The father of my little patient, by this time, had

gained admission. I heard his deep voice, in a strange language, say something. The dresser laughed.

"He says, Bwana, that it is no use putting on a bandage made from cloth, even if there is flour on it, when it needs something strong like corrugated iron or a bit of wood to keep the arm stiff."

By this time the plaster had set.

"Tell him to come and feel it," I said.

He came forward and touched the plaster gingerly. "*Yah*," he cried, "it is hard, like concrete. Surely it is magic!" and, with that, he took to his heels.

The whole native staff hugged themselves with joy. The dresser chased him to explain, and half an hour later the man went home with a match-box full of plaster of Paris, to demonstrate its virtues to his friends and relations.

With half a kerosene tin as a wash-basin, I removed the plaster from my hands, and turned to the Sister. "Anything more on the list?"

"Yes." She smiled. "There's a man here whose teeth are beyond me. I made one effort to extract a molar, without any success, and so he's come along for you to have a try."

I did a nerve block local anæsthetic, and he was most surprised to feel his lower jaw becoming numb and insensitive. The dresser stood behind the native stool, acting as a living dental chair while I performed. The bone of the African's jaw was ivory hard, and the tooth had no desire to change its domicile. However, after trying a range of forceps and elevators, I produced the molar intact, to the mutual satisfaction of patient and surgeon. We gave him a mouth-wash of permanganate, and he was horrified when he washed his mouth out.

"*Kah*," said he, "my blood has become purple."

We explained to him that that was only the medicine

to help heal his jaw. He took a bit of convincing, but at last he went away, with his tooth in his pocket, and the desire to tell everybody of a new and strange thing—a violent, but nevertheless painless struggle to remove a tooth. In the corner of his cloth were half a dozen aspirin. I explained the dosage in this way:

"How many eyes have you got?"

"Two," he replied.

"Only two?" I asked.

"Yes, only two," he replied.

"Never more?" I asked.

"No, never more," he replied.

"In the same way, two of these pills. Only two, and never more."

"Yes, Bwana," he said.

But I'm pretty sure that he swallowed the lot when the effects of the anæsthetic wore off!

The Sister and I departed for a well-earned cup of tea. As she stirred her cup, she said:

"I got a shock the other evening. Our postman had torn his shirt on the seventy-mile walk from the railway. As I took the letters, I could see a patch of leprosy through a hole in his shirt. Fortunately, it was early enough to be treated effectively. And then the cook came and said he had a similar sort of patch. It gave me rather a nasty feeling."

"You know, you ought to have a full-time doctor here. In the wet season, you have got no means of communication, and it is a hundred miles to the nearest medical help, even when the road is open."

"It is grim, sometimes, Doctor. Last year, when we were isolated by floods, we had an epidemic of meningitis. By myself, I dealt with thirty cases. Then there is the leper clinic to run, and the babies—we had 200 of them born here last year! But I think my worst moments are when a surgical emergency arises, and I have to watch the patient die, because no nurse can tackle operations of that sort."

I marvelled at the heroism of these Sisters. A hundred

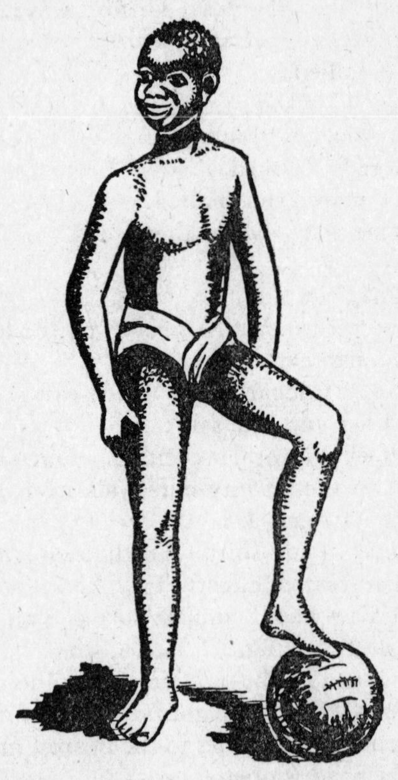

miles from a doctor, facing exacting medical problems and heart-breaking conditions, and yet cheerfully going on, thinking of the scores of successes, rather than the occasional tragedy that inevitably must come their way.

It was dusk. The mist had cleared away, and a brilliant sunset glowed beyond the mountains. I was kicking a football with the schoolboys, when a hospital nurse arrived, panting.

"Bwana, come to the hospital quickly!" I set out at the double. It was almost dark when I got there. On the floor lay a woman, scarcely breathing. She had been carried on an upturned native bed over rivers and through dense jungle, bumped and shocked in an appalling fashion. A nurse brought a hurricane lantern. Very rapidly I examined her. She had an internal hæmorrhage. Urgent operation was necessary. Her people came from a distant village, and spoke a language that neither the Sister nor I could comprehend. The dispenser acted as interpreter.

"Tell them, Godwin," I said, "that I must operate straight away. She is bleeding inside, and if we do not stop it at once, she will die."

He told the relatives, and they fell to discussing the matter amongst themselves. I had not much surgical equipment with me, so I proceeded to go over my stock.

"I will need retractors, Sister, big ones, as well as little ones. I will bend the handles of two of your dessert-spoons, if you don't mind, and then will use the handles of these hurricane lanterns, bent appropriately, for the bigger variety."

A primus had been lighted, and the instruments were being boiled in a kerosene tin, when Godwin came in.

"They refuse, Bwana. They say it is contrary to the laws of the tribe to operate unless her father agrees, and he lives four hours' walk away."

Again I tried to impress upon them the urgency of the case, but they shook their heads sullenly. "It is not our custom."

"Listen," I said. "If you have a clay pot with a tiny hole in it, and the water leaks through and all the water that you have carried from the well is being wasted, what do you do?"

"Why, fill in the hole," they said, "and the water is not lost."

"It is just so in this woman's life. Let me stop the bleeding artery and her life will be saved."

Again they shook their heads. "It must not be done. It is not our custom."

A messenger hurried off into the night to call the father. There was never a more futile journey. Two hours later I felt her pulse flicker and stop.

The relatives wailed long and bitterly. I turned to Godwin and raised my eyebrows.

"No, Bwana, it is not worth while to tell them that it was their own fault." He shrugged his shoulders. Once again the darkness of heathendom and superstition had claimed a victim.

The air was fragrant with the scent of frangipanni.

The moon rose over the Uluguru Mountains in the distance. In a low voice, the Sister spoke:

"If only we had more staff, more equipment, more drugs and dressings, we could gain the confidence of these people who live in the bush, and tragedies like this would not happen. It is only the Gospel of the living Christ that can break through this sort of ignorance."

CHAPTER VI

FLOODS, PETROL AND A TOW-ROPE

On a thick grass roof rain sounds very soft, almost caressing. I stretched drowsily under my mosquito net and had turned over to go to sleep again, when I heard Samson's voice urgently calling at the window:

"Bwana, it's raining. We must go now or we'll be here for months."

I struggled into my clothes, knocked up the Sister, said good-bye, and leapt into the car, which Samson had fully prepared for any emergencies in the mud. It was pelting down, and, even after half an hour's rain, the track was as slippery as buttered glass. Notwithstanding our chains, the old car skidded sideways, and I took my last look at Berega. I thought of the lepers I had seen and of the operations I had done, and remembered that for six months that Nursing Sister would, unaided, cope with a job which urgently required a doctor.

My musing was rudely interrupted by Samson pointing with his chin to a foaming mass of water rushing towards us down the narrow valley with a dull roar. We drove across the dry bottom and up the other side. Five minutes later the track was covered by ten feet of muddy, turbulent water that rushed down from the hills. We pushed on through a thick mist, wondering what the other valleys would be like. Fortunately, the storm water from the hills had not reached them, and we drove

out from the mountains on to the open plain, where the sun shone brightly. The plains always had a measure of excitement to anyone on this part of the safari, and that day was no exception. We rounded a sharp bend, and there, not ten yards ahead, were three full-grown giraffe. With wheels locked, we came to an abrupt stop. They looked at us curiously from their lofty vantage point, and, quite unconcernedly, turned, twitching their tails once or twice, and giraffe-galloped off into the jungle.

Samson laughed, picking up from the floor the crank handle of the old Ford:

"Now, Bwana," said he, swinging over the engine, "we will follow their example."

Two miles farther on a hundred zebras grazed on the edge of the plain, and in a sandy watercourse we came upon two hyenas picking the bones of a lion's kill. In the same river the car sank to her axles in loose sand. We put chocks under the wheels, lifted them clear of the sand, and pushed heavy timbers under the tyres, arranging them railway-track fashion in the line that the wheels would travel, then very gently we coaxed our veteran to the far bank, which we had previously cut down with hoes. Even then we required the help of three stalwart Africans, each entirely dressed in a piece of cloth the size of a pocket handkerchief.

Samson was enthusiastic: "We'll have a good safari to-day, Bwana. We dodged all that water, and so far are without punctures, and that is the last really bad patch of sand we have to cover."

I nodded doubtfully. "It's all right so far, Samsons but you can never tell what will happen on safari."

Samson shook his head: "There are not many thorns in this part of the road, Bwana, and the engine is running sweetly to-day."

I felt something of his enthusiasm, too, and thought that we would see the white-washed buildings of Mvumi hospital that evening.

Above us loomed a granite-crested ridge. A herd of gazelle lifted their heads as we approached, and trotted off into the umbrella thornbush. We crossed a rickety bridge:

"*Yah*," said Samson, "half-way to Kongwa, thirty-five miles to go," and, as if in answer, the engine stopped.

"Petrol," said the driver, laconically. He scrambled out to pour a tinful into the tank, but a minute later he returned with a rueful smile on his face.

"*Ulange* (Look), Bwana!"

He held up a tin with a hole an inch from the bottom. A nail from the box had perforated the tin, and there was only a quart or so of spirit left. We looked at each other in dismay. Here we were, in the jungle, and sixty miles from the nearest place where petrol could be bought. Quite apart from the inquisitive menagerie that roamed this part of Tanganyika, there was the thought that delays of this sort in the jungle might cost lives in a doctorless bush hospital. We had half a gallon of kerosene and a bottle of ether, but I hesitated to use this mixture, knowing the antiquity of the bus. I shook my head:

"No, Samson, there's nothing we can do about it. This is another of the times when we ask God for His help."

Together we knelt beside the bumper bar and asked Almighty God to help us. They were not eloquent prayers, but were simple and to the point, and we based our confidence on the verse which, in the African translation, reads:

"The effectual fervent prayer of a man right with God is very effective."

Then we sat down to wait.

Overhead horn-billed birds flapped and screeched. The thornbush was a mass of bottle-necked nests. Industrious little yellow weaver birds chattered noisily. A group of people suddenly emerged from a track. Their leader was a stalwart, and I recognized him at once as the African clergyman.

"*Mbukwa, Doktari* Bwana."

"*Mbukwa,* Pastor," I replied, and then told him our story.

"Oh, my son will go to Mpwapwa for you, Bwana. He will be back in four days with a tin of petrol."

I thanked him, but told him that we had prayed for someone to come along who could supply us with the necessary fuel. He shook his head doubtfully:

"But, Bwana, there has been no lorry past here for fourteen days."

I nodded agreement. "Yes, Yohanna, but let's use our faith and wait and see. I am sure God will answer."

We went with him to his house. It was scrupulously clean. His wife was grinding flour, native fashion, before the door. She got up to greet us, and then went inside to brew tea in a little green enamel kettle.

"Indeed, Bwana, I am glad you have arrived to-day," said she. "My youngest grandson has burnt his leg. I have done what you told us to do and put tea leaves on the burn, but will you see him and treat him?"

The little chap, an attractive child of six, lay on a cot that his father, the local C.M.S. teacher, had made for him from native timbers and vines. He was covered with a mosquito net, and lay with his burnt leg covered by a clean piece of cloth. His little face was drawn with pain, but he smiled bravely at me as I took off his temporary dressing.

"Bwana," he whispered, "is it going to hurt?"

"Yes, old man, a little."

"Perhaps, Bwana, I will cry a little."

I gripped his hand. "Never mind, old chap, we'll fix it up."

I sent Daudi to the car to bring up bandages and my medical bag. When he returned I produced two bottles; one was bright purple and in the other was a clear solution. The Pastor's wife had a clay pot boiling for me to sterilize the bowls and instruments. Carefully I painted the burnt area with the clear solution, and then with the bright purple dye, which greatly intrigued my little patient. While I was waiting for this application to dry, I drew him pictures on my leg with the purple antiseptic. He laughed with glee, and said:

"Is it not useful to be a European! Behold, you can draw pictures on yourself that people can see!"

Suddenly Samson leapt to his feet and ran like a stag towards the road:

"*Kah*," said my host, "why did he do that?" And then we heard the sound of a vehicle in low gear, and hurried to the road. Samson had already stopped a lorry, loaded with petrol, and was bargaining vociferously with the Arab driver.

A few minutes later Samson had filled our tank, and we had two spare tins.

"It is better to buy here, Bwana. Is it not one shilling a tin cheaper than at Dodoma?"

I smiled. "Truly, Bwana, God has answered our prayer. Not only are we able to go on, but we've saved ourselves six shillings as well!"

I turned round to my host. "Let's thank God, Yohanna. 'No lorry for fourteen days!' you said, but here we are! Half-an-hour's wait only, and all our needs supplied!"

We knelt together under the weaver birds' nests and thanked God.

"Truly, Bwana, our God is a loving Father."

"Yes," I replied. "He answers when we live our lives according to His plan."

Farewells were said, and we set out again on our safari, with a hundred miles to go.

We were making splendid time. There seemed to be a minimum of trouble, and the road wound in and out of masses of flowers. Convolvulus grew everywhere, enveloping the undergrowth and spreading up over thorn trees. The whole countryside looked as though it was covered with a vast carpet of the softest pastel shades. We skidded on a muddy corner, and drove through a mass of white, trumpet-shaped flowers with purple throats.

From underneath the bonnet of the car came an almost human cough. Poor old "Sukuma" spluttered and stopped. This was nothing new. Samson got out, went round to the back, took off the lid of the petrol tank—a tennis ball suitably incised—and blew vigorously. Then he ran round to the front, raised the bonnet, pulled sundry wires, gave the starting handle a turn, and the car burst into renewed life. We jolted forward, nosing our way through acres and acres of flowers.

At the edge of the river, Samson pulled up:

"You drive, Bwana, and Daudi and I will push." Slowly the ramshackle vehicle moved towards a wide, dry, sandy, river-bed.

"*Haya,*" I cried. "*Mukundugizenyi!*" (Push!)

They pushed with a will, as I accelerated. Then the wheel started to skid, and, when only five yards from the opposite bank, we stopped.

"Rock her, Samson," I shouted, "rock her." We swayed forward a yard. They rocked again.

"*Haya,*" I shouted again. A supreme effort from behind and then up and over, on to the sloping bank we lurched. The engine roared.

"She has jumped out of gear, Bwana," said Samson, putting a stone behind the back wheel. But she hadn't. We looked at each other in dismay. The axle had gone!

We tied a long rope to the bumper bar and dragged her a little way along the road, and then sat down as comfortably as we could, under a convolvulus-covered thornbush, to wait for someone to give us a hand. Apart from myriad flies, no one seemed to take an interest in us.

Samson cleaned the spark plugs; I read the *British Medical Journal*; and Daudi went to sleep until such time as he was discovered by a nest of red ants. He had a busy ten minutes.

Perhaps a mile away, we suddenly saw a flight of black and white ibis rise into the air and circle around.

"Someone is coming," said Samson.

We listened.

Yes, it was a lorry, and soon, across the flower-covered plains, swaying dangerously, came a lorry driven by a young Indian. He tackled the river with his accelerator flat down, but stuck in exactly the same place as we had. I untied the rope from the front of "Sukuma," and went to his aid.

"*Mbukwa*, Suliman."

"*Mbukwa*, Bwana. *Za safari?*" (What news of the ourney?)

"*Swanu du*" (Good only), I replied, following the African custom, "but we have broken an axle and cannot go any farther."

"Help me out, Bwana," Suliman laughed, "then I can tow you into Dodoma,"

For half an hour we pushed and pulled, and at last had to jack up the back wheels and put stones underneath before this skin-laden lorry got out of the river. It was piled high with cowhides, each one rolled, and the whole thing was tied down with ropes. On the top of it was perched a small African boy. He shouted encouragement as we sweated and pushed and manipulated. The final jerk that moved the lorry out of the river sent an impulse right through those coiled skins, which acted like a gigantic spring, and catapulted him into the air. He landed in a sitting-down position on a pile of sand, and joined in our laughter.

Then started a hectic thirty-mile drive to Dodoma. "Bwana, you drive," said Samson. "It won't matter

so much if you ruin the car, but if I do—ugh—there will be much trouble!"

Suliman set out at high speed. The dust rose in clouds. I could barely see the back of his lorry fifteen feet away. We swayed dangerously from side to side. Our brakes were never good, and it was a herculean task keeping that tow-rope taut. Suddenly, the road seemed to fall away beneath us. The rope slackened, and then, with a sickening jerk, we shot forward again. We had gone through a dry river-bed. The strain snapped the rope. We skidded, and came to a standstill, facing in the opposite direction. I looked across at Samson. His eyes stuck out like organ stops from his face, which was salmon pink from the dust of the road.

"*Kah!*" He laughed unsteadily. "What a journey! Who'd own a car like this?"

"Samson," I said, "I'm going to pray for a new one. I feel years older than when I set out this morning."

At that moment Suliman arrived.

"*Habari?*" (What news?) grinned he.

"Good," said Samson, "quite good. Can't you see we're facing in the opposite direction? We have got dust in our eyes, in our mouths, in our noses, in our ears. The tow-rope has broken, and I've a lump on my chin as big as a chicken's egg, where I bumped it on the wind-screen."

The Indian laughed.

The tow-rope was knotted, and we continued our journey at reduced speed.

At Dodoma I thanked Suliman very much, and produced some five-shilling notes to pay him, but he shook his head.

"Oh, no, Bwana, you saved my wife's life. You set my collar-bone, and you gave my grandfather back his sight. How could I charge you for the enjoyment of this morning?"

I left the car in the hands of George, the smiling Greek garage proprietor.

"It will be fixed, Doctor, by ten o'clock to-morrow morning."

An hour later, bathed, and dressed in a fresh shirt and shorts, I sat drinking chain cups of tea with the Bishop of Central Tanganyika. I told him the story of our safari.

"Frankly, sir, we will have to do something about that Ford. She will be the death of us yet."

"My dear boy, I'd love to give you one, but you know we've no funds here for new cars for medical missionaries. Pray about it, my son." And I did.

* * * * *

Next morning, when I went to collect "Sukuma," I found Samson under the car, checking up on the repairs.

"George," I said to the garage proprietor, "what would you give me for this car?"

"I?" said George. "Oh, no."

"It's very good-natured!" I said.

Samson's grinning face appeared from underneath the car.

"And it is very easily led, Bwana."

"Doctor, I would not buy that car," said George. "It

is worth much more to me when it belongs to somebody else. Perhaps I could sell it for you."

"I want to buy a new one, that I can use as an ambulance and in which I can carry the drugs from hospital to hospital. I want to buy one soon. What will it cost, George?"

"Round about £200, Doctor."

I could see what Daudi and Samson were thinking. They were wondering where the cash would come from. I said nothing.

As we had lurched hither and thither the day before, I had prayed, and asked God for a new car. I used this promise:

> "Before they call, I will answer, and while they are yet speaking, I will hear."

CHAPTER VII

HOME, AND A SCALPEL

"*KWETU*" (home), said Daudi, softly, as we saw the familiar white-washed buildings of Mvumi appear. Nurses and dressers ran down from the hospital to greet us. Lizards scurried away from the door of our garage. I switched off the engine. We were home.

In the late afternoon I visited the hospital, leaving orders for various treatments, and went across to the main ward. I stood outside, admiring the dresser's tomato garden, when, from the ward, came the voice of James, who termed himself "Ward Sister."

"Here comes the ambulance, Bwana."

From the noise the carriers were making, I guessed that my new patient was an adult. They came through the door into the men's ward, lowered their burden to the floor, and opened out the blanket.

"*Kah,*" said Daudi. "Bwana, this is the man that we saw at the dance near Mpwapwa."

It certainly was, and he was looking extremely sorry for himself.

"His name is Muganga, Bwana," said James.

"*Mbukwa*, Muganga."

"*Mbukwa*, Bwana," came a faint voice from the floor.

Suddenly he drew his knees up under his chin, and said:

"*Uk-k-k-k-k-k-k. E-e-e-e-e-e-e. Uk-k-k-k-k-k-k.*"

He was obviously in agony. I made my diagnosis and gave an injection to ease his pain. Daudi had his whole history, and, in his best English, he gave me his opinion of the trouble.

"Bwana, it is a case of bricks in the inside."

"Oh!" I said, "You mean stone in the kidney, or, as we call it in the medical language, 'renal colic'!"

Daudi nodded.

The patient had collapsed and was lying back in his bed. Medicines were given, a house-brick heated and tied in a remnant of blanket, and, if I had not been present, the junior dresser would have landed the whole thing, none too gently, on the tender midriff of the unfortunate patient, who was just beginning to doze. When I came to see him again two hours later he was taking a real interest in life.

I had brought my photographs to show him. He took one from me, looked at it, and for a while could not make out what it was. Then suddenly an enormous smile seemed to split his face in two.

"*Yah*," he said. "It is I. *Kah!* Am I not good looking? *H-e-e-e-e*, look at my hair!"

He rubbed his hand rather ruefully over his scalp, which was now bald as a billiard ball. James smiled, and pointed with his chin to a frangipanni tree, beneath which rested the patient's hair and its mud head-dress, which had been deftly amputated with a rusty razor.

Muganga's enthusiasm suddenly waned, and another spasm of agony racked his frame. It was obvious that an operation was necessary. I gave Daudi instructions, and he hurried off to boil up instruments.

"Bwana," gasped the patient, "I refuse that half-death medicine that you smell, that reeks of stale beer."

I wondered what the anæsthetic manufacturers would think of this testimony to their product, and assured him that he could watch all the operation, and yet would have no pain, for I had a medicine which I squirted through a needle, and that stopped pain. He was carried to the theatre. Before I operated, Samson prayed, very simply, for the man's recovery, and for help for the doctor and the dressers in dealing with the case.

"*H-e-e-e-e-e*," said the patient, "you speak as though you know Him."

"Yes," said Samson, "I know God. He is my Father. It's for Him that I work. It's to Him that I speak. We have a song better than any of those that you sing at the dances. It speaks of Jesus Christ, and says:

> He died that we might be forgiven,
> He died to make us good,
> That we might go at last to Heaven,
> Saved by His precious blood."

For an hour we operated. With a sigh of relief, I put

in the last stitches, applied the dressings, and saw him carried back to the ward. The patient weakly took my hand.

"*Yah*, Bwana, thank you. Surely *Mulungu umulungulungu* (Surely the God of Gods guides your hand). I had no pain at all."

"He is indeed the God," said Daudi. "Now, you

rest. Your worries have gone, and ours have just started!"

Next morning, I entered the ward, and came upon James, the hospital evangelist, sitting on a stool, his damaged leg in the most comfortable position, with a New Testament in one hand, and gesticulating with the other, to make sure that Muganga heard and appreciated every word. As I scrubbed up my hands, I listened to their conversation.

"*H-e-e-e-e-e*," said the patient. "Indeed it is by the help of God that I am recovering."

James read to him the story of Jesus healing the nobleman's servant. As he finished reading, James turned to our patient and said:

"Now you see how the power of Jesus worked. He was miles away from the sick man when he was made better then, and in just the same way Jesus can extend His power to you, Muganga, even if He is in Heaven. You have been helped in body, but you need more. You need to be healed in your heart. The nobleman's servant was not only healed in body, but the whole house believed in Jesus, and they were all saved from their sins. So can you be saved, if you will give your heart to Him."

"It is only the hardness of my heart," said Muganga. "I have heard the Word of God frequently in my own village, but I have not obeyed it."

I came across to him. "*Kah*," I said, "and what did you obey when you came to hospital with your pain?"

"I came because I needed help, Bwana."

"Oh," said James, "and do you not need help for your soul?"

"Feel in my pocket, James," I said.

My African friend produced a stone the size of a golf ball.

"That," I said, as I started his dressing, "was removed from inside you, and I was the only one that could do it and free you from pain."

"You see the parable," said James. "It is only Jesus that can take away from you the stone of sin that causes pain and wretchedness and suffering and death. Do you not feel the need for His help?"

A month later the African went home. James watched him walking down the winding path to the native village.

"He will never forget that practical parable which we preached to him, and he will preach it over and over again to others as he shows them the stone. Truly, Bwana, your knife preaches more effectively than your tongue!"

CHAPTER VIII

FAN-BELTS AND MALARIA

It was three months since the last thunder-storm had deluged the plains, and now there was nothing green to be seen. The baobabs were gaunt skeletons, and the thornbushes looked like gigantic barbed-wire entanglements.

The hospital was quiet for once. Following the drying up of pools, the mosquitoes had gone—and malaria with them. The people had built new houses, and our campaign for clean homes was reducing tick fever. Babies continued to arrive at the rate of two a day. Nothing dramatic was happening, nor anything very strenuous. I had brought my records up to date, and felt that everything was as it ought to be—and then came trouble in the form of a man on a donkey.

He brought a letter which told of the serious illness of an African Pastor's child, eighty miles away. It was too far to carry her in, and she was altogether too sick to walk. I called Daudi and Samson:

"Daudi, get your microscope, slides, and all the rest of it, and have them ready in a quarter of an hour. You will have to examine a blood film in the bush."

"Samson, two syringes, injectable quinine, injectable arsenic, and medicine for sleeping-sickness, also antiseptics and the emergency operation case. We shall be going in a quarter of an hour."

I threw a few necessities into a kit-bag. I could safely leave the hospital in the capable hands of the Sister. I said good-bye to my wife and small son, collected a mosquito net and a hammock, packing them on top of the kit-bag, and threw it into the back of the car, and we were away.

It was not a happy start. We were pushed half a mile before anything happened, and then, with a jerk, "Sukuma" started on her eighty-mile journey into primitive jungle.

To me it was a nightmare drive. As we bumped over rivers and drove laboriously through sand, I kept looking at my watch. I felt every hour was vital in saving the life of that child. The car seemed to crawl and the clock to race. I held my breath as we came to a particularly bad river, and prayed silently. We crossed it uneventfully, and there, in front, was the Cape-to-Cairo road. Ten miles of bone-shaking corrugations and we turned off, the signpost indicating MWITICHILA.

Six miles of dense thornbush jungle were behind us. We had been able to do it in half an hour. It was cruelly slow. Simultaneously, Samson and I realized that the radiator was boiling. He went to pour in some water, and I raised the bonnet. Imagine my feelings when I saw that the fan-belt was broken. It was almost new, and, what was worse, we had no spare. At once we set to work to repair it. We tried splicing rope, but this slipped uselessly. Idea after idea proved futile. Samson wiped the perspiration from his forehead. Suddenly a grin came over his face:

"Bwana, give me a shilling, please." I did so.

He went off through the thornbush. I strode up and down, feeling tempestuous inside. Why did this happen? Then I went round to the shady side of the car, knelt beside the running-board, and told my Heavenly Father all about it. I asked that the child might not suffer through this delay, and that we might hit upon some idea that would help us to complete the journey. I pulled out my Testament and read:

> The peace of God which passeth all understanding shall keep your hearts and minds.

I let that soak in.

Then came the sound of Samson's running feet, and, looking up, I saw him with a strip of cow-skin in his hand. With a knife, he cut it into strips the width of the fan-belt, soaked one in water, and joined it in such a way that it fitted loosely in position. As it dried, it fitted tightly. We leapt in and drove on. There were a number of other pieces of cow-skin soaking. We drove for ten miles, when there was a sharp "ping."

"It's gone," said Samson.

We hurriedly fitted another. It was just before sundown when we arrived. Daudi arranged a box for his microscope in front of the car headlights, and then hurried after me into the house.

Our little patient, wrapped in two cotton blankets, was

lying on a crude bed, made from bush timber and mattressed with strips of cow-skin, similar to those we had used as an impromptu fan-belt. Simeon, the African clergyman, gave me the history clearly, and without trimmings.

Daudi had by now taken blood slides, and was examining them. The full glare of the headlights of the car

lighted up his intent face as he peered down the eye-piece of the microscope.

The child's temperature was 105 degrees. Her neck was drawn back to a dangerous degree. She was unconscious. I made a thorough examination, and felt reasonably sure that she had cerebral malaria—malaria of the brain. I heard Daudi's voice excitedly calling me. I went out and looked down the microscope. The whole film showed blood cells alive with malaria.

I filed the neck off a special glass bottle containing

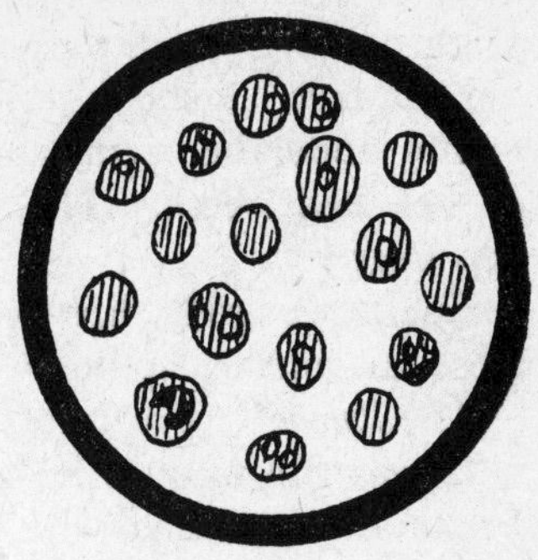

quinine for injection into a vein. Daudi held the little girl's arm while I injected. A drop of blood welled back into the clear solution in the barrel of the syringe. Daudi and I grunted satisfaction in chorus, and slowly I ran in that solution, which could mean life to our little patient and death to malaria.

The various boxes and bottles were taken out of the back of the car. I rigged up a mosquito net, took out the front seat, and arranged it as a mattress, and rolled myself in a blanket. In a moment I was asleep.

"Bwana, Bwana, come quickly!"

The anxious mother's voice was urgent. I jumped up, pushed aside the mosquito net, and hurried to see my little patient. At first I thought she had had a fit, but it was merely the tremendous shivering of a severe malarial attack. The mother brought a kerosene tin full of hot water, and we sponged her down. In the gloom behind the bed stood the father.

"Things are not good, Simeon," I whispered. Together we knelt and asked that the measures taken might have God's blessing upon them, and we asked for the life of the little girl.

"Call me at *nzogolo*" (the first cock crow), I told the mother. This was about four in the morning, and, to my intense satisfaction, I found the temperature was down to 101 degrees. Her pulse had a reassuring feel, and the neck had some slight movement in it.

When I woke again it was broad daylight. Samson had policed the area, keeping everybody quiet so that I might sleep. My little patient was lying huddled under her blanket. I shook down the thermometer and put it gently under her arm, and smiled as I felt the evenness of her heart-beat. The temperature was reassuring—100 degrees.

The little girl's lips were moving. I put my head close and picked up one word, but it was enough:

"*Nadabuka*" (I'm hungry).

It was the most cheerful thing I had heard for days. I called the mother, who was dozing by the fire.

"Marita, she says she's hungry."

She grasped my hand, and tears ran down her face. Hurriedly she poked up the fire to make thin gruel. Simeon came towards me, and said:

"What news, Bwana?"

"*Swanu, muno muno*" (Very good news), I replied. "She is conscious and asking for food."

"Thank God," he said. "Bwana, without your help she would have been dead by now. Surely God sent you to our country to help us. Are there many doctors in your country?"

"Oh, yes," I laughed, "a lot."

"Have they got cars like yours?"

"No," I said, "they have not."

"What? Do they walk?"

"Oh, no, but they have cars with polished sides and good wheels and good engines."

I looked at the veteran outside the door.

"Simeon, we nearly didn't get here, and, if we hadn't"—I shrugged my shoulders.

It was Sunday morning, and I watched the people trooping across the plains to the little mud-brick church. All the furnishings were made from packing-cases. The people sat on the floor. The place was soon full to

capacity. I was brought a stool, and sat in a special corner. Familiar hymn tunes were sung tunefully to African words. The service was most enthusiastic and sincere.

Simeon's sermon was typically practical and to the point.

"Behold," said he, "last night I saw the Bwana preach a sermon with a microscope, a bottle of medicine, a syringe and a needle. My daughter lay dying. Never have we seen a child recover who has been ill as she was ill, but the Bwana came, took blood from her finger, and found the cause of the trouble. It was not witchcraft, but a *dudu* in her blood. He prayed, and then squirted medicine into her body through a hollow needle. The medicine looked like water, but tasted like the juice of a thistle, and behold, this morning she asked for food! Nothing but that medicine could have saved her life, and, truly, my friends, it is a picture of what Jesus did for us on the Cross. Only His death could pay the price for the disease of sin in our souls. Are we not thankful to the Bwana for helping our children? Should we not be more thankful to the Son of God for giving us Everlasting Life?"

I was most intrigued to see the people bringing their gifts. Instead of a collection plate going round, each man and woman brought up his or her offering. Some had corn cobs, some millet seed, some ground flour. Each was put into a different receptacle. A sombre-looking man stood holding a round basket, into which eggs were put. As each was brought, the name of the donor was written on it, and I was more than amused to see, after the service, that a dish of water was brought, and the eggs were tested. Two were bad, and I saw the church officer disappearing on the war-path to interview those who had given them.

I spent two or three days on the spot making perfectly sure that the little girl was on the way to complete health. On the third morning she was well enough to come to the door and wave to us as we moved off on our way back to Mvumi.

CHAPTER IX

TWO AND FOUR MAKE . . .

"OLD 'Sukuma's' going like a bird to-day, Bwana," said Samson. "I cleaned the spark plugs, put in new bits of wire here and there, and removed very much dust from the carburettor. While you mended that small child, behold, I tonicked the car."

I laughed at his queer English, but the laugh turned to a groan. There was a horrible crunching noise, and, with an almost human screech of pain, the old car stopped. I looked at Samson. He made a wry face. We were at least fifty miles from anywhere, and that appalling noise in the vitals of the old car was ominous. We got out, pulled up the floor-boards, and in so doing liberally bespattered ourselves with grease and dust, only to find the gear-box was damaged beyond our ability to repair it.

"*Kah*," said Samson, "we can do much with string and wire and bits of cow-skin, but the gear-box, Bwana, is beyond us."

I nodded. "We are quite useful at make-shift, Samson, but this is a different matter. There is only one thing for it. We will have to walk home, and get George to come out from Dodoma later on and tow poor old 'Sukuma' to his car hospital."

Daudi had been taking his bearings. With his chin he pointed towards a clump of baobab trees. "There is a C.M.S. School over there, Bwana. I will tell the teacher of our difficulties, and he will get the small boys from his class to drag the car to his house, and he will look after it for us."

He moved off through the thornbush. A few minutes later a score of African children came running towards us. They stopped to greet me. One came to show me his arm, which had been broken.

"Look, Bwana," said he, "this is the side that the witch-doctor burnt with a glowing stick and poulticed with mud and manure."

I looked at a mass of livid scars, a testimony to the medicine man's thoroughness. He pointed to the other side.

"This is where you put your white powder which became hard as stone when it was wet. Eh, and your pills took away the pain."

Another little lad pulled down his eyelid. "See Bwana, my eyes are well now because of your blue medicine."

A small girl was standing with her mouth open, making strange sounds, and I realized she was showing me where I had extracted one of her teeth.

All these little folk were extremely friendly. Some

grabbed the rope tied to the front axle, and heaved. Others got behind and pushed. The old car moved forward to the accompaniment of cheers and a queer sort of a chant, as they dragged us to a little clearing outside the mud-and-wattle school.

"*Assante, wadodo*" (Thank you, children), I said, and went over to see the old teacher. He was most keen for me to have a look at his school. I walked with him through the doorway and looked at the little building, which was neat, and very obviously a school.

"How long have you been teaching here, Hezekiah?" I asked.

"I have been with the Church Missionary Society for twenty-two years, Bwana, and here for fifteen of them. I'm still teaching the children. They are those who one day will lead our tribe, and perhaps all Africa. I am the old man who builds the foundations. They don't show much, but, Bwana, they matter greatly."

The whole equipment was a blackboard, the back of which bore the stamp of a well-known brand of petrol; a tin with some stumps of chalk; three native baskets of small stones for the arithmetic lesson; and half a dozen well-thumbed New Testaments.

Outside were a number of squares of ground, all duly sanded over. Each square was our equivalent of an exercise-book. Writing was taught, and two and four, after due cogitation, made six!

"Bwana, you arrived just as we were doing hygiene," said he.

"Show me how it goes, Hezekiah."

A little boy was given the order: "You be the tick." He ran inside, and soon came out again on all fours with a small brown mat tied to his back. The children broke into song. It was the old tune of "Three Blind Mice,"

but the words in Chigogo told of three bad ticks tha were the carriers of the deadly relapsing fever. The lived in somebody's sleeping mat, and were very happ till its owner went to school, and learnt that ticks dislike sunlight. As verse followed verse in brisk dialogue, th ticks complained of the heat, and, while scampering int the shade, were pounced upon by the children, wh crushed them with their feet. At this stage, a concerte

rush was made on the little fellow disguised as a tick, and there was a terrific scrimmage.

Hezekiah smiled delightedly. "It is thus, Bwana, tha they learn to keep well. How much work I can save you at the hospital if we can stop the children from getting ill."

Samson appeared round the corner of the school-house. Over his shoulder were our water bottles and some food and clothing. Into a small suitcase I packed the string hammock, a rug, and a few necessary medicines.

"Well, Hezekiah, we must leave you now. There is a fifty-mile safari in front of us. I'm thankful that the country is mainly flat and there aren't many lions about."

"Not many, Bwana? Why, last night, in the village over the hill, two cattle were killed, and an old man, along the road that you must travel, was killed a week ago by a man-eater!"

Daudi grinned. "We'll walk only in the daytime, I think, Bwana. We'll stay in the houses of the people at night. If you sleep in your hammock, insects will find it hard to reach you."

The children walked a little way with us, and then waved good-bye as we set out on our long foot safari across the plain. It was glaringly hot. Thornbush were the only trees in sight. The ground was parched, dried and cracked. We walked in silence until we came to a mass of granite boulders, giddily balanced one upon another. In their shade were the bones of a lion's kill. Overhead hovered three great vultures. We did not stay to investigate, but walked on, hour after hour, making always for a conical hill on the horizon. Stopping under the shade of a huge rock, we could see a cloud of dust

rising as hundreds of hump-backed cattle were driven slowly home from their grazing ground.

Daudi pointed with his chin towards a group of huts. "Bwana, let us stop at this village for the night. To-morrow we can start well before sunrise and travel in the cool."

I was more than willing to stop, and was most relieved when we reached a number of flat-roofed mud-houses, built in a clump of baobab trees.

CHAPTER X

TICKS AND TROUBLE

THE Chief came forward to shake hands. We went through the whole elaborate ceremony of Gogo greeting, and then told him of our broken-down car, and of our need of a night's rest. Immediately he offered his house for us to sleep in. We accepted gratefully. Three-legged wooden stools were brought out, and we

sat in the shade of a baobab, all the time doing battle with myriads of flies; it was obvious to me where they came from. The Chief's house was typical of the "tembe," or mud huts, of the local people. It was high enough to stand up in, and perhaps ten feet wide, the actual house being built round the central cow-yard. The richer a man is, the greater will be the pile of manure in this enclosure, and the odour of his house is thus an indication of his wealth! I couldn't help wishing that my host had not been so well off.

I walked into the house to have a look round. Where I was to sleep was quite apart from the quarters of the family. In the gloom of the mud hut, with its mud roof, its mud walls, and its mud floor, I could dimly see two great wicker-work bins. As my eyes became accustomed to the gloom, I saw a fat rat move cautiously from behind one of these and scamper off into the darkness. Three monster cockroaches were disturbed by him, and scuttled off under some cooking pots. In a corner was a hen and three chickens, and beyond her were great stone jars and a mixed collection of gourds and pumpkin shells, used for the water-drawing process.

Carefully, I knotted the ends of the hammock to the strong posts that held up the roof, arranged my blankets and mosquito net. The atmosphere inside was rather overpowering. The cattle had been driven into their enclosure, and although you could not see them, the goats and the sheep were making their presence felt, even in the darkness. My eyes smarted from the smoke coming from the primitive kitchen, where my host's wife was cooking the inevitable evening meal of *ugale* (porridge). At the low doorway was a small boy, filling in time by digging fat ticks out of cracks in the wall with a long, sharp thorn. I shuddered as I saw these insects; a bite from one of them might well mean death to a European.

After satisfying myself that the hammock was tick-proof, I went for a stroll through the village with the Chief. He told me of the prospects of early rain, and how they expected this year to be a phenomenal one for rainfalls. We were passing an enormous baobab tree at the time, so large that its base was bigger than the average bandstand. Looking up into it, I saw three coffin-like affairs tied amongst its gaunt branches.

"What are they?" I asked. "Have you been burying people and putting them in a tree?"

He laughed. "*Zoochi du.*"

"*Zoochi?*" said I. "*Zoochi?*"

Samson smiled, and, in English, said: "Bees, Bwana, bees!" It was rather different from what I had expected.

The Chief took Daudi aside and whispered in his ear. My African friend nodded and laughed. Mystified, I followed them. At the extreme end of the village was an enormous tree. Probably, it had been growing there for a thousand years. Slowly we walked round the base of it. It was easy to understand how the baobab had been called the "bottle tree." This one in particular looked like a gigantic ginger jar. In its trunk was a hole big enough to crawl through.

"Look inside there, Bwana," said the Chief.

I peered inside, but could see nothing. Samson struck a match, lighted a handful of grass, and threw it inside. Once again I put my head through the hole. My cry of surprise echoed eerily in the great hollow tree. There, staring up at me, and looking inexpressibly ghostly, were a dozen human skulls. Whitening bones filled the interior of the tree. Although I had seen this weird sight before, I pulled my head out hastily.

It was a nice prelude to my night's rest. An hour later, I carefully swung myself into the hammock. I adjusted my mosquito net and lay, waiting for sleep to come. The atmosphere was thick with smoke and the aroma of goats. My host and the family had gone to bed. This

merely consisted of wrapping themselves in a blanket. They carefully covered their heads, but left their feet sticking out. From away in the forest came the roar of a lion. The cattle stirred restlessly in the *ibolulu.* I twisted convulsively and nearly fell out on to the floor. When all was said and done, it was not a very comfortable night. At four in the morning, the family rooster felt it was time for him to make his presence felt. His crow coincided with a particularly vivid dream, and a few seconds later I picked myself up ruefully from the floor. My night's sleep definitely was over.

I dressed and walked outside, just in time to see the Chief, clad only in a loin cloth, pulling from his person the great glutted ticks, as big as the large joint of your thumb, which had feasted upon him that night. He counted them as he pulled them off, and crushed them beneath his feet. When I arrived he had reached the "forty-one, forty-two, forty-three" stage.

Samson had rolled up the hammock and my blanket, and we were about to move off on our long safari, when an ear-piercing scream, "*Ooo-iwi-iwi,*" came from the other end of the village. A woman rushed frantically out of a house, clasping an infant in her arms. She rushed to the Chief's house, and in the half-light before dawn, I saw the emaciated body of a five-year-old child. He was breathing tremendously fast and was obviously dying.

"He's been bewitched," cried his mother. "Did you not hear the hyenas last night? Were they not sent by my mother-in-law to bewitch him? She has cast spells on all my children, all five of them. Are they not all dead?"

Samson touched me on the arm.

"Bwana, take a blood slide. There is much in this story that you do not understand. You are a European, but I, an African, understand."

From my medicine-case I took a glass slide as large as a tram ticket, pricked the child's finger, and took a drop of blood. Smoothing this over the slide, I stained it purple. A minute or two later, the child twitched, and died. His mother picked him up and fled into the jungle, wailing dismally. There was a sinister hush. The Chief had disappeared, and only a crow perched in the baobabs broke the silence.

Samson drew me aside. "The Chief wants to see you, Bwana." Together we went to his "tembe." In a dark corner sat the head man.

"Bwana," he whispered, "can you tell if that child died from *Wuhawi* (witchcraft) or not?"

"Indeed I can. That drop of blood that I've got

here will tell a story when I look at it under my microscope."

"We will come in three days' time to make a *shauri*—to discuss the matter. You will know by then, Bwana?"

"Oh, yes, I'll be able to show you then."

With muttered farewells, we set out. The sunrise was a blaze of colour, the early morning breezes were cool and refreshing. In silence, we walked through the maize gardens and out again into the plains. Samson came level, and said:

"There you are, Bwana, that's Africa—fear, ignorance, witchcraft and death."

"And yet, Samson, there are people in my country who say: 'Leave African people alone, they're happy enough as they are.'"

"But they don't know, Bwana. They've never seen what we've seen to-day, and surely they've forgotten the slave trade days and the days when the Germans killed my people."

"I'm afraid, Samson, that's just it; they've forgotten."

We walked on in silence for miles; it was too hot to talk. The track wound through a dense piece of thorn-bush jungle. The trees met overhead, and in front of us were a number of holes, two or three inches deep, and big enough to hide your hat in.

"Those," said Samson, "are rhino footprints."

"Are they recent, Samson?"

"I hope not, Bwana. I do not like the rhinoceros. It puts its head down, sticks out the spike on its nose, and charges right through the jungle, through thorns, crashing down everything in its way. It'll toss you with its horn and then trample on you with its great feet."

There was a crashing in the jungle behind us. Samson and I looked round apprehensively. Behind us we could see the trees swaying as though they were being broken down. I felt a tightness in my throat. Samson's eyes were nearly popping out of his head, and then we saw a dozen great baboons swinging through the underbush. Seeing us, they stopped, stood up, and let out that peculiar bark, which can easily be confused with the roar of a lion.

"Monkeys!" Daudi spat. "And we thought it was a rhino. Bwana, do you know how to dodge a rhino?"

"No," I said. "It should be a useful thing to know in this jungle. What do you do, Daudi?"

"Wait until he is perhaps three yards away, coming at you like an express train. Then you very swiftly jump to one side, and he crashes on, and can't stop. Then it's time to run!"

"Huh, it's a nice story, but I'd hate to stand there and wait for him to get close enough."

Samson suddenly grunted, and deftly pulled a great thorn out of his heel.

"Punctured!" he grinned. "I hope the teacher out there"—he pointed west with his chin— "is looking after our poor old sick car. Bwana, why do missionaries always have old cars that break down?"

"Well, Samson, when ten shillings means a person's life saved, you don't feel like spending money, except on the greatest necessities."

"But, Bwana, you have wasted two days walking through the jungle. That might have been a rhino, and then there'd have been no more Jungle Doctor!"

"I know, Samson, but then, we trust in God to protect us, and we can be sure that He will."

"Bwana, I wish that some of the people in other lands, whose cars run on concrete roads, and who do not have to steer by compass, and whose tyres are never punctured by thorns, and who never have to stop their cars because of lions in the road . . ." He paused for breath.

"Well, what do you wish they'd do, Samson?"

"I wish they'd send us £200 for a new car. One we could use as an ambulance, Bwana. It would mean fifty lives saved a year, and days and days and days of your time saved. *Kah!*" he grunted, and pulled out another thorn.

"That's what I'm praying for, Samson. Wishing's a waste of time; praying isn't."

Out of the belt of thick jungle, we came again to the open, scrub-covered plains. Seven miles away, on top of a small hill, the sun shone on the white roof of the hospital. It was very heartening to feel that you were in sight of home. I almost forgot the blister under my heel. We took a brief spell, sitting on the roots of a great baobab.

"Samson, tell me about this *shauri*. By the way, what exactly is a *shauri*?"

"Anything that has to be discussed, whether it's a court case, a quarrel, a wedding being fixed, or a dispute over wages. Anything like that is called a *shauri*. We Africans love them. Is it not an excuse to sit down?"

I laughed. "But tell me about this one we are going to hold the day after to-morrow."

Samson carefully ticked off the points on his fingers.

"In the village where we were this morning, Bwana, we saw a small boy who died. His mother says that he was bewitched by her mother-in-law. The mother-in-law says it's a lie."

"Samson, you've forgotten the bit about the hyena. The mother said that the mother-in-law had sent the hyenas to bewitch the child, but the mother-in-law denies it."

"Yes, Bwana, but the mother says that all her children

have died because the old women have bewitched them. There will be many strong words said. The mother will tell her story. Her relatives will back it up. The old women will tell their side of the story. The Chief and the elders will listen to it all, and then you put your 'fly into the ointment'."

"You've got the wrong proverb, Samson," I laughed. "In English we say, 'You throw your spanner into the works.'"

"Daudi and I will help you, and we'll prove to the people that this matter was not witchcraft, but ticks. You've got that slide safely in your pocket, Bwana."

I opened my notebook, and there was a scrap of glass with a stained smear of blood upon it. Samson smiled.

"*A-a-a-a*, it will be good to prove to them, to let them see with their own eyes, what the trouble is."

We were on the last stage of our safari. We trudged up the last hill to my ramshackle home. I sank, with a sigh of content, into an easy chair made from packing-cases.

"Where's the car?" asked my wife.

"Out in the *mbargo*" (jungle). "Gear-box went bang, so we had to hoof it. Mile after mile of forest, and then this scorching plain in the blinding sun. How I wish we had a decent chariot instead of that partly animated collection of spare parts."

Mary poured out a cup of tea, and smiled: "I'm glad I wasn't with you, for the children's sake."

"So am I. It was no place for a woman or a family. I had to sleep in a hammock, and was nearly eaten by ticks. A packet of monkeys gave us quite a lot of thrills on the way through that stretch of forest near Mwitichila, and Samson and I both thought there was a rhino about. It's great fun to look back on it, but, oh, it's good to be back. Anyway, how have things been on the home front?"

"Oh, life hasn't been free from thrills. Matteyo, the gardener, fished a live cobra out of the well this morning. Kefa took a jigger out of David's toe, and the cook got mixed up between the salad dressing and the condensed milk!"

We both laughed.

"*Malenga ga baf tayari* (Bath's ready), Bwana," said my house-boy.

I pulled myself to my feet, and had a shower under a combination bucket and watering-can, strung up to the roof, got into my pyjamas, and stretched luxuriously.

Two days later, people started arriving for the *shauri*. The Chief came with two of his special police, each armed with a *kiboko*—a dangerous-looking hippo-hide whip. I entertained him to tea. He was passed a plate of scones, and, following native custom, he motioned to his clerk, who picked up a small basket, and tipped all the scones into it. I was a little taken aback. My cook saw this, and smiled. He scribbled on an old envelope and handed it to me. I read: "Please, Bwana, do not worry. They were stale ones."

I was given the seat of honour in the grass-roofed *shauri* house. The Sub-Chief arrived and regaled the audience with the story of my investigations inside the baobab tree. Daudi arranged his microscope, bottles and glass slides carefully in a corner of the room. The mother started to tell her story. She began quietly, but became more and more worked up.

"*She* did it!" She pointed her chin accusingly at the mother-in-law, who sat, sneering, on a three-legged stool in the front row. "She has bewitched all my children. Did she not send the hyenas to howl outside our house?

Doesn't the Chief know it? Doesn't the Bwana know it? Do we not all know it?" Her voice rose to a shrill scream.

The Chief stopped her. "Tell us your story," said he to the old woman.

"*Kah!*" said she. "There is nothing to tell. Bewitch her children? Of course I did nothing of the sort! It might have been others, but it certainly wasn't I! Is there any profit in bewitching your own grand-children?"

An old man, with enormous ear-lobes, filled with bead ear ornaments, got to his feet, and told of prowling hyenas, of charms found outside the house, of the wild talking of the old women.

Another ancient took a sniff of tobacco snuff, and told his version. He believed that the mother had been drinking and had not cared for her children properly. There was a storm of disapproval at this. The Chief ordered the native policeman to eject one of the relatives, who was shouting at the top of his voice. Things were becoming distinctly hostile, when Daudi had his say.

Turning to the Chief, he said:

"Oh, great one, I can explain the death of this child."

A hush fell on everybody. Daudi took a bayonet-pointed needle and some cotton-wool, soaked in methylated spirits, and pricked the great man's finger. He took a drop of blood, stained it, and arranged it under the microscope.

"Listen, my friends! The Chief is a strong man. He is well. He has no sickness."

"Truly," agreed the audience.

The Chief closed one eye and looked down the eye-piece of the instrument.

"*Yah*," he said, "I can see little round, red things."

"That," said Daudi, "is your blood. Can you see anything but red things?"

He focused up and down. "Nothing," said the Chief.

Daudi took the slide that I had taken from the dying child, three days previously.

"This is the blood of the child who you say was bewitched. Look at it."

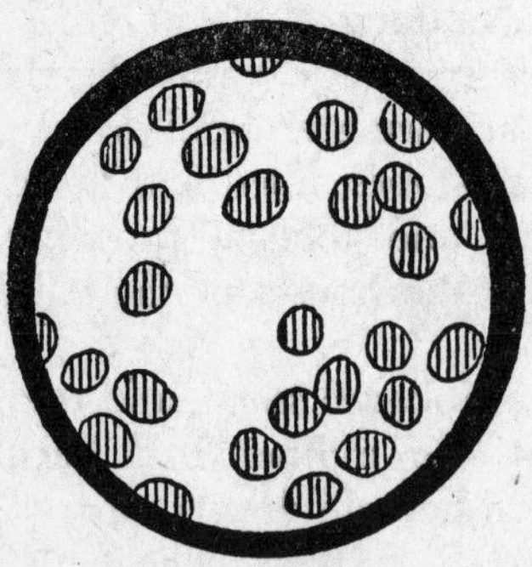

NORMAL

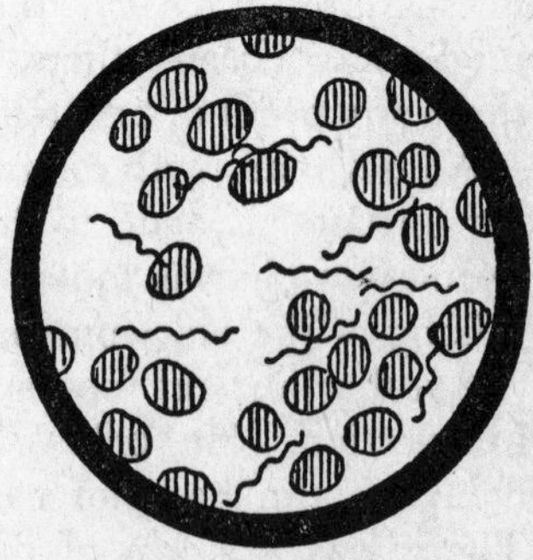

TICK FEVER

Again the Chief peered through the eye-piece.

"*Yah*," he said. "There are the red things, but there are also purple, corkscrew-like things. What are they?"

"They," said Daudi, dramatically, "are the reason why the child died. He was not bewitched by hyenas. He was bitten by ticks. Those purple things you see that look like small corkscrews are the germs of a fever that you get when you are bitten by a tick."

He whipped round upon the old woman.

"It's your fault the child died. You should have swept your house."

He turned sharply to the mother: "It's your fault, too, that your child died. You left him to lie on a cow-skin on the floor."

Turning to the Chief: "It's your fault, too, for not making all the people of our tribe follow the wisdom that is taught by the Bwana doctor, and by all the other missionaries. Let our teachers give you the words of truth about insects and disease, and mothercraft and fathercraft, and then your children will not die. Witchcraft!" There was scorn in his voice. "Oh, when will you turn from the ways of fear to the Way of Life? Listen . . ."

In their own language, he quoted the verse which we had read that morning at staff prayers:

> Fear thou not, for I am with thee. Be not dismayed, for I am thy God.

The Chief took me aside. "Truly, Bwana, we have had our eyes opened. I will back up your work as never before. Bwana, continue to train our youths so that they may help us as Daudi has helped us to-day."

I gripped his hand.

"That's what we are here for, Chief."

CHAPTER XI

FIRE AND FAUNA

THE train pulled up with a jerk.

With difficulty, I got to my feet and jumped from the guard's van to the ground. Six hours in a Tanganyikan goods train is a mixed experience. I glanced at my watch. It was three o'clock, and the station was deserted, but for an old friend, the Nyasaland stationmaster, who spoke English with a Glasgow accent. He looked at me, grinned, and said:

"Sorr, there'll be no carr the dee. It'll be wauking that ye'll be."

I thanked him, and turned to my companions.

Samson already had my suitcase on his shoulder. I put the instruments under my arm, and Daudi arranged the sundries on a pole over his shoulder. It was only a twelve-mile walk, and I vividly remembered my previous experience on that same safari, when, driving along in an Arab's ramshackle lorry, we had come face to face, first with a black-maned lion and then with an immense lioness. I turned to my companions:

"—*Ale cibete*" (Come on, let's go).

We set out cheerfully enough in the bright sunlight, and walked along the narrow track cut through the wild jungle that skirted the track like the sides of a railway cutting. It was intensely hot. I mopped my brow as we stood in the shade. Before us was a stretch of road a mile long. I pointed with my chin to a place almost up on the top of the next slope.

"It was there, Daudi, that, on our last safari, we met the lions."

"*E-e-e-e-e-e*," he replied, "Roger told me that story."

We walked on, each one of us thinking his own thoughts.

There was a deep roar from the forest in front of us. I stopped involuntarily. The roar was followed by some piercing shrieks.

"*Zinyani du*" (Only monkeys), said Samson, but we were ali feeling a little bit on the stretch.

We topped the hill with its lion memories. Before us was another stretch of road, almost identical with the one just covered, but, lying in the middle of it, some half-mile away, was a great tree trunk.

"*Nhembo*" (Elephants), said Samson. "Behold, two years ago, on this road, a car stopped while they chopped through the trunk of a tree like this one, but before they could move it out of the road, four elephants arrived, and became busy with the car. They smashed it up into little bits, and the driver was lucky to get away with his life."

I fell to whistling "Home, Sweet Home," but I am afraid the point was not appreciated by the Africans.

The sun was beginning to set. We had still three miles to go. The sunsets are marvellous in these high plains of Tanganyika, where you are only a few hundred miles south of the Equator. The sky changed through oranges to reds, to deep purples, and finally a peculiar green shade. The trees overhead cast fantastic shadows, knob-billed birds cried eerily as they flapped overhead. We came to the top of another rise. I flashed my torch ahead, and my heart almost stood still, for I could see a glow coming from behind a rock. It was deep red in colour.

"Samson," I whispered, "what colour are lions' eyes at night?"

"Red, Bwana," said he.

"Well, look at that!"

We huddled closer together and looked at this weird phenomenon ahead of us, and then I laughed. It was nothing more mysterious than someone fiddling with a tail-light. The local C.M.S. missionary was lying under his car, tinkering with a faulty universal joint. Our stuff was quickly bundled into the back of his car, and soon we were able to help. A quarter of an hour later we were on our way to Kilimatinde. We drove through the Arab town, past the usual mud-brick shops, through a grove of palms and mango trees, and pulled up before the white-washed Mission House, relic of the days of German control, with its huge walls, its wide windows, and its low doors. Masses of purple bougainvillia grew over the veranda. Thankfully, I sat down in an easy chair and looked with approval at a man-size cup of tea.

"Oh, Charles, it's good to sit down. I left Dodoma this morning just after breakfast, and had to sit on a bag of sweet potatoes in an unsprung goods van. My only companions were two crates of chickens, which included a politically-minded rooster."

My friend laughed.

"I was coming to meet you, but the old car broke down."

"Old car! It's the same thing everywhere you go here. I had to be towed in my wretched old bus behind an Indian's lorry, and then the garage man insulted me by offering me a fiver for it. And there's your Chev here, that had done sixty thousand before the speedometer broke, and the Bishop's vehicle, to quote a Scotsman, is worse than anything he had seen in Aberdeen."

Thoughtfully, I put down my cup, and was looking round for a second when I heard a wild yell from outside.

"Bwana, *nzoka*, *nzoka*!" (snake, snake!)

Charles leapt to his feet and rushed out of the door, gripping a pea-rifle. I collected a stick, and followed at the double. By the light of a hurricane lantern, I could see Daudi jumping round excitedly outside the garage door, throwing stones under the car. We could dimly see a hooded cobra. We dragged the car out, and there was the ugly-looking reptile, five feet long, looking extremely ferocious. I could see another car up on bricks at the far end of the garage, and I recognized it as belonging to a missionary on leave. Charles had the rifle to his shoulder. He pulled the trigger. The bullet hit the snake and ricocheted, whining across the room, and tore its way into a full petrol tin. The spirit gushed out. Charles fired again, and this time the creature fell,

mortally wounded. Daudi, lamp in hand, dashed forward to administer the final blow with a stick. But it was never struck, for, in a split second, the whole place was a mass of flaming petrol. The snake was forgotten. I seized the shovel that was against the wall, scooped up some sand, and flung it on the flames. Charles dashed in, and, with the utmost bravery, seized the petrol tin, and, flaming as it was, threw it through the door. I was terrified that the second car would catch fire, but, after two minutes of desperate fire-fighting, everything was under control, and we turned our attention to the snake once again. It lay paralysed, but still alive, in the centre of the garage, but not for long. Daudi had an extensive burn, and Charles's nether garments would never be the same again!

I dealt with the African lad, and, on my return from the hospital, found Charles and his wife waiting for me.

"I thought, Doctor, before turning in, that we might spend ten minutes thanking God for His care."

Taking out a worn copy of the Bible, he read the 91st Psalm. Thought after thought gripped me as he read:

> "He that dwelleth in the secret place of the Most High shall abide under the shadow of the Almighty.
>
> "Thou shalt not be afraid for the terror by night. . . . Nor for the destruction that wasteth at noonday. . . . There shall no evil befall thee, neither shall any plague come nigh thy dwelling. Thou shalt tread upon the lion and the adder . . ."

My friend looked up from his reading:

"Here's the reason for God looking after us, don't you think?" And he read again:

> "Because he hath set his love upon Me, therefore will I deliver him."

The sincerity of my friend's prayer as we knelt, gripped me. He thanked God for protection on that journey, on a road that probably sees more lions than Englishmen; for protection from fire and from venomous snakes. I got up from my knees, and gripped his hand.

"Yes, Charles, the only worth-while thing in life is to give yourself into God's hands, and to leave yourself there."

I got into bed, carefully examining my mosquito-net corners for any stray malaria-carrying insect, and tried to go to sleep. It was not easy. Hyenas were making the night hideous with their cries, and there was a lion somewhere out beyond the hospital. When I did fall asleep, my dreams were tinged with red eyes, that suddenly burst into flame, and hooded cobras. It was not a restful night. I had promised myself the next day off. I would leave my mind fallow for a few days before making a hundred-mile safari into some of the wildest country in East Africa.

CHAPTER XII

FEVER, FLIES AND A FIGHT FOR LIFE

As we got up from breakfast next morning, Charles said:

"How about spending an hour or so looking round the old German fort?"

We set out together and walked down a long avenue of gorgeous flame trees. Their brilliant red flowers lighted up the dim interior of the Arab shops with their strange conglomeration of cotton blankets, peanuts, wire ornaments, and hurricane lanterns. Closely-veiled Arab women moved furtively around in the deep shadows behind the shops, and small children with shaved heads played in the litter in front of the houses. The road itself had been built in the days when Tanganyika was German East Africa. Beyond us stood the wreckage of what had once been a German Seat of Government. My companion gave me a stick.

"This place is alive with snakes," he remarked.

First, we came to a sentry-box near the main entrance that was now blocked by a thornbush. The sentry-box still had the remnants of red, white and black paint upon it. We scrambled up the walls and saw where Belgian shells had torn their way into the fort in 1917. On each corner of the place was a battlement with loops for rifle or machine-guns. The walls were four feet thick, and built of stone. What stories they could have told of

Germans, with hippo-hide whips, and sweating Africans linked together in the chain-gangs, carrying stones and mixing lime mortar! My companion pointed beyond the wall, beyond the edge of the cliff that rose one thousand feet from the plains below. He showed me the faint outline of a road that disappeared in the heat haze of the plains of Ugogo.

"That's an old German track, Doctor, built of stone, two feet above the level of the plains. It was an all-weather road, and a remarkable achievement, but the people here tell me that it was built not so much with stone as with the blood of Africans. More than five hundred people perished in the chain-gangs in the building of that road."

My interest was turned again to the inside of the fort. There was a central courtyard, where once had been gallows and whipping-post. Now it was full of weeds and vermin. I picked up a piece of crumbling sandstone from the wall, broke bits off, and tossed them into a tangle of vegetation in a far corner of the ruins. One of them, to my great surprise, started a hyena from his lair. This sinister creature let out a shrill howl and slunk off.

We explored the whole of the place, and saw in particular a corner that had been used as the first Church Missionary Society hospital. A very make-shift affair it has been, but it seemed fitting that the place which had seen so many German atrocities should be used as a hospital in the early days of the British Administration of Tanganyika, to relieve the ills of the thousands of people who live in the area.

We walked together down the side of the mountain pass, and came to a look-out that gave a splendid panoramic view of the plain below. As we stood there, identifying various landmarks, my friend pointed out a group of

Africans five hundred feet below us, who were extremely excited over something. We could see messengers running post-haste in three directions. An old woman was hobbling from a native house with a shallow gourd, which we knew would contain butterfat. There was something in the centre of that ring of people that was exciting them intensely. I sent Daudi post-haste to bring my binoculars from the hospital. I had never seen anything like this before. In the centre of the group was an old bearded man with a red blanket round his shoulders, whom we recognized as the Sub-Chief. He was keeping the people very quiet, and their interest was riveted upon some queer incantations which he was making. Hurrying down the narrow path from Kilimatinde village came the Chief, and behind him a big group of Africans. We watched them with interest. They hurried down to the level of the plain, and stopped still on coming to the group of people. The ranks opened up to let the Chief into the centre. He put a gourd to his mouth, tilted his head back, and swallowed. At this juncture, Daudi arrived with the glasses. Rapidly I focused them, and watched the scene intently. The Chief took another mouthful of milk, and then carefully spat the whole of it upon what looked like a collection of sticks on the ground in front of him. The Sub-Chief put his hand into the greasy native butter, and seemed to be anointing the sticks, which appeared suddenly to lurch forward. I handed my glasses over to Charles.

He looked long and earnestly, and then whistled:

"It's an *itumbiko*" (A native sacrifice of some sort).

Daudi asked to have a look.

"*Yah*," said he. "*H-e-e-e-e-e*, Bwana. Behold, this is a strange thing. It is a stick *dudu*. An insect that my people worship. Oh, it is considered to be a good omen.

Bwana, let us go close and see. Behold, I have brought your camera."

Regardless of the thorns, we pushed our way down to the old German road, and hurried to watch proceedings. Everyone was so preoccupied that they did not notice us,

and we climbed on a group of rocks where we could have a very full view of all that was going on. There was the stick insect, eighteen inches long, and so exactly camouflaged that you could pass within a yard of it without realizing that it was not just a broken branch of thornbush. There was actually a thorn-like growth on its back, and it swayed strangely to and fro on its queer, twig-like legs. Its tail had been carefully anointed with butter. Daudi whispered that this was a way of pleasing

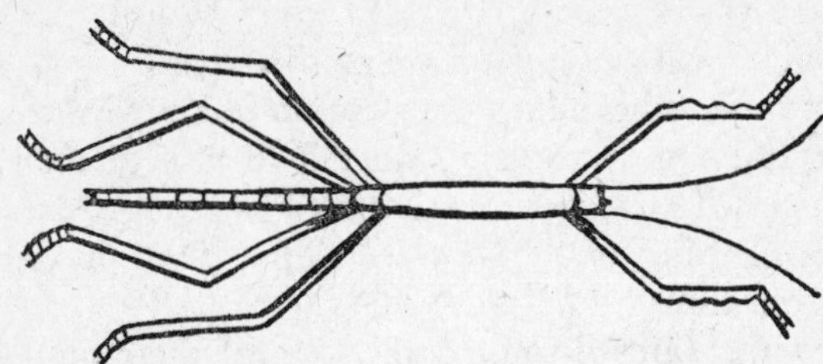

it. Its head was damp with the milk that had been skilfully spat by the Chief, who was now making a speech, addressed to the insect. It was not so much a prayer, but rather a request that the rains might be given. He walked round the creature, asking for fertility for the soil, and good crops; that their herds might be strong and produce well, and that they might be kept from illnesses.

I got my camera into position and took a picture. The click of the camera attracted someone's attention, and we moved down amongst the group. The proceedings, apparently, were over. We came very close to the insect itself, and examined it:

"Do not touch it, Bwana," said the Chief. "It is a very bad thing to touch one of those. They are very powerful."

"Would you object," I said, "if I photographed it?"

"Oh, no, Bwana, as long as you do not drive it away."

In front of the creature we put a sheet of newsprint, and it most obligingly walked on to it. I put my camera to good use. On each side of the creature were queer folding wings. Suddenly it flapped these and flew off, alighting on the roof of a mud house. The owner clapped his hands with glee, and rushed off to put a gourd of milk in front of it.

"*O-o-o-o-o, A-a-a-a-a*, this is a good thing!" he cried. "Behold, I will have good crops this year."

My friend, who had a very intimate knowledge of the people and their language, started to talk to them, and the Chief, who was in an extremely good mood, explained to us something of African worship. They have many strange customs.

When the rains do not come, one of their practices is to sacrifice an all-black calf, or, if this is not available, a goat without one single white hair. The creature is killed by cutting its throat, and its blood is offered. He was not quite sure to whom. He said they chose a black calf, because they felt this would encourage black clouds to come up, and black clouds meant rain.

"And what happens to the calf or to the goat?" I asked.

"*A-a-a-a-a-a*," said the Chief, "we eat those, Bwana."

As we sat there talking, my friend told of God the Creator, and of sin, and how the Son of God had come down to earth to be a Man and pay the price of sin.

The Chief shook his head.

"It is hard to understand, Bwana."

One old man came forward and said: "Bwana, why did God send Jesus, His Son?"

Before I was able to reply, Daudi said:

"Bwana, let me explain. These people will understand me, because I am one of their own tribe, and yet I am also one of God's tribe."

We both nodded. He turned to the group standing watching the insect.

"Listen to my parable. Behold, near our C.M.S. hospital at Mvumi I have a garden, and in that garden I plant peanuts, and each afternoon, when my hospital work is done, I go to dig my garden and to plant my peanuts, and with me goes my dog. The first day I had finished planting one row, and I saw my dog digging them up again, so I came across to him and said: 'Stop it!' and shook my finger at him and looked fierce. The dog looked guilty, and wagged his tail. I explained it to him. 'Do not eat those peanuts. They are not good for dogs, and if they are not left in the ground there will be no food for me,' and I thought he understood.

"But next day I found him digging there again, so I slapped him and said: 'Don't do it. Would you bring famine upon your master?' The dog whined, and I felt sure he understood that time. But the next day, as I planted, behold, he started to dig again."

"*Kah*," said one old man, "I'd have thrashed him."

"Yes," said Daudi, "that's just what I did. The dog howled, put his tail between his legs, and looked as miserable as a dog can. In a very fierce voice I warned him, but it was no good. Next day, he was digging them up again."

"*Kah*," said the old man, "a worthless animal!"

"Well," said Daudi, "I knew one more thing I could do. So next day, when I went to dig in the garden, I took with me a piece of meat, and, as he started to dig, I whistled him to me and gave him the meat. 'Good dog,' I said, 'this is better food than peanuts.' He leapt up and took the meat out of my hand, wagging his tail furiously. 'At last,' I said, 'he understands.' But next day he was digging the peanuts up again."

"*Kah*," said his audience. "What could you do? The dog was hopeless."

"Yes," said Daudi, "I sat in the shade of a paw-paw tree and thought, and, as I thought, I said to myself, 'Behold, it is a very great problem. The only way I can make this dog understand is for me myself to become a dog, and to speak in dog's language. Then, and then only, can I make this stupid creature understand.'"

"*Kah*," said the old man, "but you could not do that."

"No," said Daudi, "but that's the point of my story. God saw that we men were very hard-hearted and very dull-headed. He tried all sorts of ways to make us understand about sin, and its consequences, but we would not listen. So He did what we could not do, and He Himself became a Man, and became poor as we are poor, lived as we live, felt as we feel. He died to take away our sins."

There was silence for a moment, and then a man, who had not spoken before, said, very quietly:

"God, who made the world, we cannot understand. He is too vast. But a Man we can understand. We know what He looks like."

Daudi nodded. "Jesus, who was both God and Man, was nailed to a tree by men, and paid the debt of your sin and mine."

Shadows were lengthening as we said good-bye. I heard one man say:

"Our offerings are given, but to whom do we offer? Would it not be better to follow the Jesus way?"

We had climbed the winding German-built track from the plain to Kilimatinde village in bright moonlight, and then had goat chops for dinner. We sat down to a game of chess. Ruefully I watched a knight go, then my queen, and then I was check-mated. Charles laughed. "Better urn in now. There's a hundred-mile safari before us o-morrow, Doctor, and the road is a nightmare. I'll vake you at five."

"Righto, Charles," I replied. "I've got my operating :it ready, and it's only a matter of a few bottles of ether ınd we'll be set. Good night."

In the brilliant starlight I walked across to my room hat overlooked a hundred-mile view of the plains, on vhich lived a hundred thousand people. It was my ›ractice! Our hospital was the only medical aid o this vast collection of people. It was a colossal task.

I got into bed and carefully tucked in the mosquito ıet. Then I knelt and thanked God for help given, and ısked His help for the coming safari. Before turning ›ut the light, I read, as was my custom, some verses rom the Good Book, and I came upon an old friend—one ›f those promises that anyone who has given his life com›letely into God's hands can always cash in upon. I ·ead it out aloud:

> "I can do all things through Christ which strengtheneth me."

I blew out the lantern and went to sleep, secure in the :nowledge that I had standing with me, in this work, he living Son of God.

Next morning we drove off, when no one but the local ·oosters was taking an interest in life. We made the nost of the first ten miles, on a reasonably good road. The sun was rising as we descended the steep pass that vound its way down the side of the Rift Wall, to the ›lains below. Looking over the side of the car, the lriver is encouraged to be cautious when he sees below :he wrecks of three lorries. It seemed to me that the vag who had nailed the bottom of a petrol box, inscribed

"*Pole, pole tazama chini*" (Go gently; look down), had evolved an excellent scheme to ensure careful driving down a highly-dangerous strip of road.

Now we were on the plains, driving through groves of stunted palm trees. In front, standing out green against the sun-scorched plains, was a large plantation of mango trees, amongst which were a number of Arab shops, and beyond it a little mud-plastered building with a rude cross above it. We pulled in to pick up the African clergyman, Benjamin, who was coming with us on safari.

I got out of the car and walked over towards his house. From inside came a mournful wail —the sound made by the *Wagogo* (the local tribesfolk) when someone has died. Grabbing my medical bag, I ran towards the house. I had a feeling that I could be of help. At the door I met Benjamin, looking the picture of woe. He grasped my hand.

"Oh, Bwana, a woman from the bush was on her way to the hospital. It is a forty-mile walk. She arrived here last night, and behold, her baby is born, and it is dead! It is her seventh child, and they have all died, and she did hope that at our hospital she might be helped this time."

I hurried past him to where I saw a new-born baby lying on a piece of folded blanket. It was not breathing, but when I put my hand on its chest I found the heart was still beating.

"When was it born?"

"A quarter of an hour ago, Bwana."

"Benjamin," I cried, "I want hot water quickly."

"We've none, Bwana, not a drop."

From my medical bag I pulled an ear syringe, and had wrenched some rubber tubing from my stethoscope. Charles appeared at the door.

"Charles," I said, as quietly as I could under the stress of things, "I must have hot water at once. Drain the radiator. Go like smoke. There's a life at stake!"

Benjamin grasped the baby by the legs and held him upside down.

I put the rubber attached to the ear syringe into its throat, and sucked back violently. The child's chest heaved. At last its air passages were clear. Hastily I filled a hypodermic syringe, and injected its contents into the quivering little body. Benjamin's wife had arrived with a kerosene tin full of cold water and a dried pumpkin shell dish. A minute later Charles appeared with half a bucket of rust-stained hot water. I scooped up a dishful of this and poured it over the child, and followed it quickly with one of cold. Everything depended on the next few minutes.

"Samson, work that throat-clearing syringe."

"Charles, pour hot and cold water alternately over the child; don't mind me, I'm going to do artificial respiration."

Both my companions complied with a will. I grasped the little arms and compressed the chest rhythmically.

In the background stood Benjamin and his wife; three little black girls peered round the corner of the house. The baby's grandmother crouched in the shadows, muttering.

Less than a minute later, the child coughed, spluttered, and then let out a lusty bellow.

Samson beamed. I relaxed my efforts, and, picking up the child, carried him across to his mother, who lay on a native bed in another room of the native house. She was lying with her face to the wall, in utter dejection. Benjamin's wife had made her as comfortable as she could. I came across to her. She didn't open her eyes

Without a word, I handed the baby to a native girl behind her, and felt the woman's pulse:

"*Uli muswanu?*" (Are you all right?) I said.

She shook her head.

"Bwana, my heart is heavy. My joy is finished. Behold, my child is dead. If only I could have got to the hospital in time! The Pastor prayed, but God did not hear. Oh, indeed, my life is useless!"

Benjamin stood at the end of the bed. He was a very short man. Above him towered my Australian friend. The little African started to speak:

"But, truly, God did hear our prayers. Even while we were praying, the Bwana, who comes here perhaps once every year, was at the very door. He has been working."

"*Kah*," interrupted the woman, "but what good could his arrival do? The child was dead. It was not breathing."

"No," said Benjamin, "but it is now."

The woman whipped round, and, seeing her infant in the arms of the smiling girl beside me, she could say nothing, but put out her arms to the child. There was a moment of very intense silence, and then Benjamin summed up all our feelings, and thanked God that we had arrived at the moment of greatest need. His wife whispered to me:

"Do not worry. I will see that she and the baby get to the hospital."

The woman grasped my hand and kissed it.

"Thank you, Bwana. Surely God sent you. Surely He is God Almighty."

When we got out to the car again, Samson was refilling the radiator. Daudi was getting as comfortable as he could in the back, and making room for the little African Pastor.

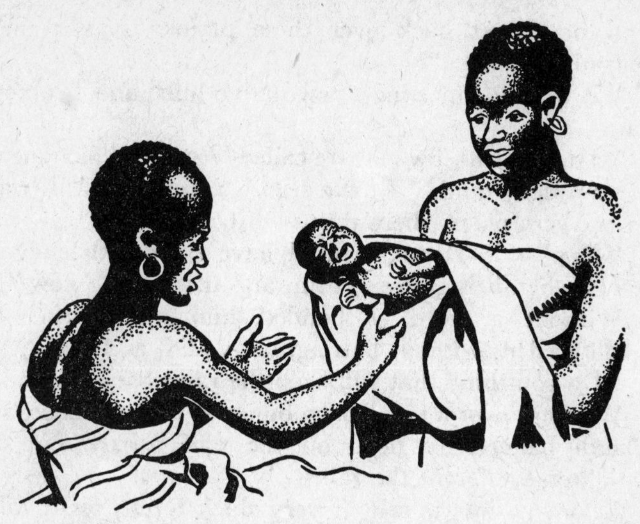

Charles let in the clutch, and we were away. We turned off the main road, and drove most carefully mile upon mile over plains which shimmered white in the glare of the equatorial sun. There was a thin layer of salt on top of the hard-baked and cracking earth. There were stunted patches of thornbush here and there, and occasional straggly groups of palm trees. It was not scenic country.

"*Kah*," said Daudi, "when it rains these plains are a swamp. You sink up to your knees in mud, and, Bwana, do not forget that the baobabs were green early this year! Perhaps in a fortnight what is now hard ground will be a bog, and you will have to leave your car right out in the forest and walk home."

My friend dexterously changed gear, and said, in English:

"It is true enough, too. If the rains come early we

will never get back over these plains. It is a most fearful mud-hole."

We were just passing a few native huts, and Benjamin said:

"These plains, Bwana, are called '*Itetema*,' which means 'Very sticky mud.' I have seen a man sink to his waist in the very place where this road is."

"*Kah*," said Daudi, "and I have a tooth that always aches when it is going to rain, and it is aching now."

Without a word, I handed him an aspirin. He swallowed it, without batting an eye-lid, and said:

"Do you think that will keep the rains back, Bwana?"

We went over a very sharp bump at that moment, and Daudi banged his head on the roof briskly. In our laughter, we forgot the rains.

Before us was a belt of very thick forest, eight miles across. The thermometer was well over 100, but before entering this belt of closely-packed thornbush and heavy timber, we stopped, put up all side curtains and blocked every available crack that opened into the car. It was stifling inside. The glare of the plains gave place to a strange twilight as we drove through the very dense jungle. In places it closed in over the road.

"*Mhola, mhola* (Gently, gently), Bwana," cried Daudi, warningly.

There was a screeching of brakes, and simultaneously the radiator seemed to disappear, and we shot down a slope into a dry river-bed. It was almost impossible to see this sudden drop in the road. On the other side, the river bank seemed to rise sheer, but we struggled up it in low gear.

"*Wow!*" said the driver. "I'd hate to drive up that hill if the banks were wet."

We were hardly out of that difficulty when the whole

car seemed surrounded by a swarm of bees. They banged up against the windscreen, and, notwithstanding our careful blocking of every entrance, somehow they got into the car.

"*M'bung'ho*" (Tsetse fly), said Benjamin. "*Yah, Zikusuma kuluma*" (My, they can bite!).

Daudi was streaming with perspiration and swatting vigorously at these agile insects. I felt a sharp stabbing pain in my shoulder, and yelled in surprise: "Eh! What's that?"

"*M'bung'ho*," said Daudi, convulsed with laughter, but a split second later he leapt into the air, cracking his head a second time on the roof, and made a statement which I can best translate:

"*Yah*, Bwana, I am bitten underneath!"

But as rapidly as we had entered this tsetse fly belt, we were out of it again. I picked up from the floor one of the insects which I had slaughtered. It was as big as a March Fly, and had a striped body. There was another one on the windscreen, fortunately outside, and I noticed that the creature had folded its wings in rest.

"Nasty brute," said Charles. "It feels like a red-hot hat-pin being stuck into you, doesn't it?"

I nodded. "Sometimes I wish I wasn't a doctor."

"Why?"

"Well, I know the symptoms of sleeping-sickness that these brutes carry. First, the glands of your neck swell, then you get a fever, and then you get progressively more drowsy, and, without treatment, all sorts of paralysis, and—good-bye."

Charles grinned.

"How can you tell if you've got it or not?"

"Microscope," I replied. "Take a blood slide, stain it and, if you see a nightmare sort of apparatus that looks like a sausage with a sail on it, then you're a candidate for triparsimide, an arsenic preparation which kills the wog all right, but also occasionally produces total blindness."

"Nice programme," commented the driver.

We took down the side curtains, killing any stray insect that had found sanctuary in the dark corners of the car.

For the last ten miles we had not seen an animal. No buck could survive the attacks of these vicious insects.

"The only creature that seems to be able to stand up to the bite of these brutes is our old friend, *ndogowe*" (the donkey), laughed my friend.

"Oh, well," I replied, "that's fortunate, because they bit me."

CHAPTER XIII

LAST LAP

My month at Kilimatinde had been rather varied. It included an earthquake, a murder, and a severe bout of asthma. I was back at Mvumi, and had had a busy first afternoon with five cataract operations to do. Walking home from the theatre, I stopped to talk to Samson, who was arranging spanners on a petrol-box shelf fixed into the mud-brick wall of our empty garage.

"Well, Samson, before long we will have a new car."

"What, Bwana, have you the money?"

"No, but I have the faith. I have asked God for a new car, and I have a feeling here"—and I pointed to a spot two inches south of my ribs—"that He will supply what I have asked Him. There's poor old 'Sukuma' with her gear-box in a knot right out there"—I pointed with my chin over the plain. A large lizard looked at me unblinkingly from the rough floor of the garage. I threw a twig at him. He scampered up the wall. I looked at him warningly:

"You must be careful, my friend," I said. "Before long, this place will be dangerous for lizards. We'll have a brand new car, which can be used as an ambulance. It will have big wheels and strong springs and super-shock absorbers. Grey lizards cannot be seen on grey floors."

The lizard blinked, and Samson laughed:

"But when, Bwana, when?"

A cheerful voice was singing in the thornbush behind my peanut garden. It was the postman, carrying over his shoulder the mail-bag. I took it from him, unlocked it, and sorted out the various letters, and proceeded to open my own. The first one asked intimate questions about my digestion, and contained a reply-paid card for a sample. The second was a quaintly-phrased letter from an Arab patient. The next was a bill for hospital

blankets. The last was a very ordinary-looking envelope, and the letter it contained was brief and to the point:

> DEAR DOCTOR,
>
> I have credited to your account the sum of £200, and I feel sure that you need something in the way of an ambulance over there. From all reports, your present car is not all that it might be. I believe God wants me to send you this, and I hope you will find it useful.

Without comment, I handed my wife the letter. She moved closer to the lamp to read it.

"*Hodi*," came a voice at the door.

In walked Daudi and Samson.

"Bwana," said the latter. "Here is the bad news. 'Sukuma' has ruin in her gear-box. She will never go on safari again."

Before I could reply, my wife passed the letter to the two Africans.

As they read, their eyes seemed to stick out.

"*Kah,*" said Daudi. "It's come."

"Come on, everyone," I said. "There's only one thing to do."

We knelt together, and thanked our Almighty Father for supplying us with a car, which would mean scores of lives saved, would remove the nightmare uncertainty of unreliable transport, and bring much freedom from unsought, time-wasting adventure to a Jungle Doctor on Safari.

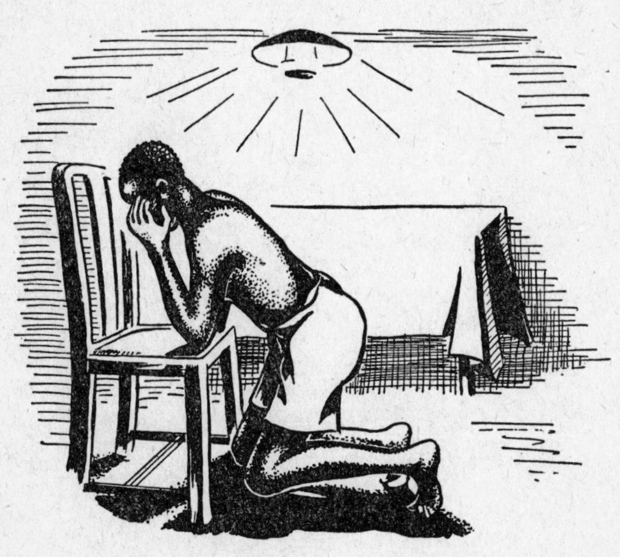